The Christ Story

*One of six books of Questions
a series of explorations*

William Corlett and John Moore

The Christ Story

BRADBURY PRESS SCARSDALE, NEW YORK

The authors are grateful to E. J. Brill, Netherlands, for permission to quote from *The Gospel according to St. Thomas* © E. J. Brill, 1959.

3 2 1   82 81 80

Library of Congress Cataloging in Publication Data
Corlett, William. The Christ story.
(Their Questions)
Summary: Examines the ways in which the sacred writings of Christianity deal with fundamental questions.
   1. Christianity—Essence, genius, nature.
[1. Christianity] I. Moore, John, 1932– joint author.
II. Title. III. Series.
BR121.2.C635   1979   201   79-15687
ISBN 0-87888-150-6

This book is one of a series.

The titles are *The Question of Religion*, *The Christ Story*, *The Hindu Sound*, *The Judaic Law*, *The Buddha Way* and *The Islamic Space*. The books were written in the order as listed, but this in no way implies any suggested precedence of one religion over another nor any preference on the part of the authors. Each book may be read in its own right, rather as each note of an octave may sound alone.

However, for an octave to be complete, it depends on the developing frequency and character of each note. In the same way, it has been the experience of the authors, approaching this series as one work, to find a similar development as they progressed from one book to another.

One

It is reported that, nearly twenty centuries ago, in a corner of the Mediterranean world, in a country that then—as now—was known as Israel, a certain man was born.

If the reports are correct, his life spanned a mere thirty years or so. And his death, and the events that followed immediately after it, are shrouded in a strange, magical atmosphere only rivalled by the stories about his birth and about the deeds said to have been performed during his life.

The man was named Jesus; and he is also called the Christ—"the anointed one".

*

Of his short life, not a great deal is known. Until the age of twelve there is a handful of stories about him; then he disappears into obscurity, only to emerge again about three years before his death.

It is these three final years—sometimes spoken of as his "ministry" —that inspired one of the great faith-religions of the world, the one that we know today as Christianity (and by "faith" we mean an absolute trust by those who believe).

Twenty centuries . . . and still the man called Jesus Christ is worshipped, loved, respected and revered throughout many lands across the entire globe.

*

Who was this man?
What was it that he said or did that is so vitally important that

those who believe in him say that he still "lives" and that his message is as essential and as pertinent now as it was when he was "in the world"?

*

His coming into this world, it is claimed, was miraculous. He was conceived without sexual intercourse having taken place. He was born to a humble peasant girl who remained a virgin. Her husband was a carpenter and, although he was not the father of this child, it appears that he cared for the infant and brought him up as his own child.

The birth took place in a stable and it was here that the infant Jesus was visited, according to different reports, by kings from far countries and by shepherds from the hills. The visitors worshipped and adored and brought gifts as though he was a "king" himself—or as though he was a divine being, for they believed that he was the fulfilment of ancient prophecies which spoke of the coming of a Messiah, a saviour, who would change the lives of all who listened to him and obeyed his teaching. In fact, he was to be a man who would give answers to the deepest questions of mankind and an understanding of the enigma that we call life.

During this man's ministry, he gathered around him a small group of devoted followers; to them he spoke. He told mysterious stories; and his followers, in turn, told of mysterious acts that he performed. They said that he turned water into wine, that he gave life back to the dead . . .

Finally, it is reported, one of his select group of disciples—a man who had loved and revered him—betrayed him to the Roman authorities who regarded him as a subversive revolutionary whose activities were not in the best interests of the state.

After a mockery of justice and the degrading of his image in the eyes of the people, he was brutally executed—by being nailed through the hands and feet to a wooden cross, at the summit of a little hill called Golgotha on the outskirts of Jerusalem, and being left to hang there until dead.

*

It is a poignant and haunting story.

It would be hard for anyone not to be impressed, and perhaps moved, by it.

And it does not end there.

*

Three days after this man had died on the cross and had been taken down and laid in a rock tomb, some of his followers came to prepare his body with all the customary ceremony given to the dead. Despite the tomb having been sealed, the body had disappeared.

Later, this same man, who had been seen to die, is said to have visited his followers and spoken to them. They saw him and touched him. And they believed that he was alive again.

They claimed that he had "risen from the dead".

He instructed them that they should go to all parts of the world and tell people what they had seen and what they had learnt; and for those who listened and believed the Christ story, there would be forgiveness of their sin and, after death, they would live eternally.

And after he had spoken to them for the last time, Jesus, the Christ, disappeared. He was "taken up into heaven" . . . and they saw him no more.

*

That, very briefly, is the story of the Christ. It will be familiar to all those who have read the Christian scriptures.

*

Did he really ever exist?
Did someone invent the story?
Could a man be miraculously conceived?
Could a man die and come back to life again?
Who was Jesus?
Who is the Christ?

3

Why is the Christ story so powerful that it should have attracted millions of followers over two thousand years?

We are asked to "believe in him"; what is this mysterious capacity called "believing" and why do we do it?

The Christian tradition speaks of "sinners"; what is a "sinner"? Who can be justified in judging another man a "sinner"?

And all those enigmatic stories called "parables" that he is reported to have told; what are they saying?

What is it all for?

What does it all mean?

To me, now.

What does the Christ story *mean* . . . to *me*?

*

If I stop to consider such questions, and many others like them —and by "stop" I mean ceasing to chase round in my mind, ceasing to take for fact those things that I have believed to be true because so many of the people around me believe them . . . if I do stop this assuming and this habitual believing, then I discover a curiously relieving experience—one of not knowing. I simply *do not know*, for certain, any of the answers.

I realize that I have heard and read—and have believed or not believed. I realize that I have assumed, however vaguely, that it has simply been a case of accepting, rejecting or ignoring reported *facts*.

I begin to wonder how and why I came to believe what I have believed. And I see that as I grew up I was subject to many assertions, persuasions and vague explanations—but no totally, absolutely undeniable answers. I was led into belief when my mind was innocent. Above all, I was led to believe that I could *learn* the truth.

*

People believe many things; they also disbelieve many things. This believing and disbelieving is necessary, for the mind needs a standpoint; it needs to establish a structure of belief in order that

4

the individual's actions can be justified. Sometimes, especially over "matters of principle", people believe and justify very strongly; they will fight and argue for the sake of maintaining their adopted standpoint. They have, in countless thousands over the centuries, even been prepared to die rather than forsake their beliefs.

But what is this "believing"?

When I stop to consider what I believe and disbelieve, I see that ultimately such adopted viewpoints have much to do with my desire to establish myself as an individual; to ensure that that individual is identifiable by others; to justify that individual's place in the world—his or her existence and survival. Once established, the individual becomes committed to the structure of belief and, such is the desire for security, the mind becomes loath to modify or abandon the structure.

What other people believe is their concern; it is not my business—providing they do not seek to impose those beliefs and their consequences on me against my will, nor threaten the survival of society at large by seeking to impose them on that society by subterfuge or force.

Let me find strength then to examine and question my beliefs if I wish to do so; and, if others wish to join me, I am happy that they should.

If we find that we disagree, then let us agree to disagree! Why should I expect someone else to agree with me—unless it be to enhance my own self-esteem?

But if we find that we agree, then undoubtedly there will be a bond of understanding between us.

*

There will be some who will say that no good can come of asking such questions as "Who is Christ?" or "Who was Jesus?"

"Such questions will get you nowhere," they will say. "You simply have to have faith, to believe. It is unbecoming (disrespectful, blasphemous, heretical, presumptuous, useless, sacrilegious) for a man to ask such questions."

5

But why?

Because they have never dared?

Why should I be given the capacity to question and then be forbidden to use it except for mundane matters?

Why should I not be allowed to exercise it in this most crucial of quests?

Providing I am prepared to accept the consequences of my enquiry, why should I not explore the greatest of mysteries?

How did it come about that the religious factor—a most significant one for the well-being of the human psyche—should have become so shrouded with taboos and mystique?

One reason must be that, once the doctrine of a religious tradition is established, any attempt to question it is seen as a threat and, hence, gives rise to a fear and resistance in the minds of those who hold office in it and those who have committed their belief to it.

*

Those who have committed their belief to a particular religious dispensation may be extremely fortunate in being blessed with such a capacity for faith—or they may be desperately blind and immature. Who is to say?

Why should I, or anyone else, be blessed because I happen to be able to believe something; and, equally, why should I be damned if I find I am unable to believe something?

Who, ultimately, is the judge?

Must I not question in order to understand for myself? How else can I be sure of my peace of mind?

*

This book is written as an exploration.

It is an exploration for we who write it and, we hope, for those who read it.

But it will only be a meaningful exploration if we are all—both readers and writers—willing to enter the labyrinths of our minds to find out what has been and is going on there.

6

The Christ question (quest) is not intended solely for those who wish to confine themselves to the Christian tradition, or for those who are just idly curious about it. It is one of many stories which relate to the human experience called "spirituality". In the particular context of this book, we are making the exploration through some of the words used in the form of religion known as Christianity.

*

One of the reasons for attempting this exploration of the religious phenomenon is that there are signs that man has now reached a stage in his evolution where he apparently is willing to abandon religion in its established sense; where he is increasingly confident to challenge dogma and superstition; where he is willing to question on a scale that is perhaps unprecedented in recorded history. The fact that states are now being founded on powerful, atheistic, materialistic, political ideologies suggests that this is so.

This emergence from dependence on the "god-idea" may be extremely foolish and ultimately catastrophic for humanity; or it may signify the beginning of liberation into a new era. It may mean that minds are becoming fatally self-delusive; or it may mean that they are developing a more advanced understanding of the human condition. *We need to know.* We need to examine what we, as humanity, are moving into. We need to ask again, with urgency, what man is and what his purpose is. Only by doing so can any alternative "philosophies of life" evolve, reasonably and consciously. No process stands still and, assuming we do not think we have "arrived at perfection" already, it would be ignorant to think that we have no responsibility in the matter.

History demonstrates that such developments do not happen spontaneously. They emerge from a combination of inspiration (and, we may ask, where do inspirational ideas come from?) and individual people—you and me—asking themselves questions and realizing certain things about their present condition. They inevitably start by asking themselves what they believe and why they believe it.

It is crucial now for me to know whether I can dispense with my idea of "god"—if, that is, I already have accepted such an idea; if I have not, then ought I to acquire one?

Is the acceptance of the existence of a deity simply a way of avoiding certain responsibilities?

How can I understand the deep longings and questions within my heart and mind?

If the established "faith" religions are dying because they no longer satisfy man's intelligence, and if the man-invented, atheistic ideologies are suicidal, what new "religion" might evolve to meet the "higher aspirations" of the human psyche?

*

If I awaken from the habitual dream I have about myself, I observe that, because I am ordinarily so absorbed in the everyday traffic of my life, I do not give much attention to the spiritual aspect. I may go regularly to religious places and take part in religious ceremony—but do I stop to consider what I am doing and why I am doing it? Possibly it all seems so unfathomable that I do not attempt to find out; perhaps I have tried and failed.

But what does religion mean to me?

According to where I was born and the environment in which I grew up, so I may have been introduced to a certain form of religion. I gather that, basically, my religion (and any other religion) derives from the proposition that there must be an unmanifest cause or creator of this world—a god, or gods, known by many names. I learn that, according to my particular tradition, spokesmen through the ages have decreed certain laws by which a man must abide in order to live a worthwhile and fulfilling life. And, finally, I gather that obedience to the law and doctrine of that religion provides certain insurance concerning death and "after-life".

It is a very tempting package!

All I have to do is believe.

*

Let us suppose that I am born into an environment where I am introduced to the form of religion called "Christianity".

I learn that its inspiration arose from the reported existence, sayings and activities of a man named Jesus. Because he had such impact and influence on a number of his contemporaries, and because of what they believed about him, he came to be called the Christ.

The reports of Jesus's life are contained in writings which originated some twenty to seventy years after his death. Four of these accounts came to form the first four books of the New Testament—the Christian part of the Bible.

The first three of these accounts (known as the Synoptic Gospels and attributed to St. Matthew, St. Mark and St. Luke) give a fairly similar story; the fourth (attributed to St. John) is a very different account in many respects.

Among the accounts not considered authoritative and not contained in the Bible is the so-called "Fifth Gospel", attributed to St. Thomas.

There has been considerable debate over the centuries as to the authenticity and meaning of these scriptures. Thousands of books have been written expounding theories, explanations, interpretations —and often not for purely objective, theological reasons. We should also take into account that in the course of being handed down to this century, the text has been translated through different languages.

So heated has been the debate and so divergent the opinions regarding these writings that the original Christian Church (the collective name for the followers of Christ) has divided numerous times during its growth over the centuries so that now, within the Christian faith, there are many different sects (Roman Catholic, Eastern Orthodox, Protestant, and so on), each subscribing to particular interpretations and beliefs about the meaning of the injunctions and teachings.

Naturally, each sect would claim that its interpretation or emphasis is the most accurate and relevant; and though by implication

9

each would therefore judge the others "less true", they would nevertheless presumably claim that the Christian religion is the one "true" religion. And again by implication this would mean that all other religions are "less true". However, in recent times, such claims to exclusivity and superiority have become more muted as many believers of the different faiths have begun to feel the need for unity, if not of belief, then at least of common purpose. For "the hordes of the heathen" are increasing and the differences of approach to religion need to be put aside as religion itself comes increasingly under siege from atheistic ideologies.

In considering the Christ story then, in the face of a bewildering proliferation of claims and refutations, doubts of authenticity, dubious criteria for selection of the "official" scriptures, translation through different languages, varied interpretations, beliefs and opinions, how can we hope to be sure of a reliable meaning?

We may say that that is what this book is trying to discover.

*

We could say that it is out of the question to expect that there could possibly be an absolute, definitive meaning which would be *the truth* of it. Even if there were, I would still then have to believe it; in other words, however "true" the interpretation, it is still a question as to whether my mind can accept it.

So, we come back to asking: "What does the Christ story mean to me?"

What is my mind looking for in it?

What are my feelings about it?

*

God . . . Trinity . . . Father . . . Son . . . Holy Ghost . . . Virgin Birth . . . Baptism . . . Sin . . . Repentance . . . Heaven . . . Hell . . . Crucifixion . . . Resurrection . . . Ascension . . . Eternal Life . . . Forgiveness . . . Love . . . Atonement . . . Grace . . . Judgement . . . Communion . . . These are some of the words or expressions associated with the Christian tradition.

Regardless of what they may have meant as words in whatever language throughout two thousand years, what can they mean to you and me *now*?

Is it possible to understand them without being asked to believe something which cannot be shown to be evident . . . *in our own experience*?

∗

As we begin our exploration, it is as though we are entering a labyrinth into which there are several paths that we may choose to follow.

We may seek out some trustworthy, devout Christian—one who already "believes"—and ask him or her to expound their belief and instruct us. But will that be of any help? Not if all they can offer is the exhortation to believe. However much and whatever it is they believe belongs to them; they found that belief for themselves; we have to do the same.

If we are to rely on our own intelligence, then where do we look?

If only Jesus was alive, then we could hear him speak and we could question him in person. But two thousand years separate us. And supposing he never in fact existed historically? Does it make any difference if the story was invented by other men? It is the story we have to be concerned with.

So, supposing the story was not meant to be taken literally; supposing the life of Jesus is, say, symbolic and the meaning of it is timeless?

Would that not be just as telling?

If all we have are the scriptures, then it is with them that we must begin our search. There, in the Gospels of Matthew, Mark, Luke and John, we will find recorded the story of the life of Jesus; there we will find recorded the stories which Jesus told; there we will find the stories that his followers told about him.

And let us not forget the fifth book, even though it is not officially accepted as part of the authentic canon. Discovered in Egypt about thirty years ago, the Gospel according to Thomas, comprising

11

one hundred and fourteen "Sayings of Jesus", is a strange, enigmatic fragment. It lacks the continuity of the other four—it is not a story and cannot be read as history. But the parallels between it and the other four are undeniable and it has its own distinctive element to add to our exploration.

So, in these five books we may hope to find fleeting images, terse hints and flickering glimpses of the Christ message.

*

Jesus—the teller of stories.
His disciples—tellers of wonderful stories about him.
Christ—the story, telling of the living man, a divine being.

*

Jesus said: Know what is in thy sight, and what is hidden from thee will be revealed to thee. For there is nothing hidden which will not be manifest.

(Thomas, Log. 5)

What can that mean—to me?
(Jesus said:) *Who hath ears to hear, let him hear.*

(Matthew, 13:9)

Two

In the beginning was the Word, and the Word was with God, and the Word was God.

The same was in the beginning with God.

All things were made by him; and without him was not any thing made that was made.

In him was life; and the life was the light of men.

And the light shineth in darkness; and the darkness comprehended it not.

(John, 1:1–5)

With these majestic—and well-nigh incomprehensible sentences —the Gospel according to St. John begins.

*

What *on earth* can they mean?

Is there anyone, anywhere, who is absolutely certain what those sentences intend? If so, how would I know for certain that he knew? And would he be able to tell me so that I was certain that I understood them?

How can I possibly understand them?

Would they help me to understand what religion is?

Who was St. John?

Was he just a poet, "a seer"? Did he make up the words? Why did he choose to express himself in this way?

On whose authority does he make such a bold assertion?

If they are the first, and obviously crucial, lines of one of the key scriptures I am to rely on to introduce me to the Christ message—

a message which St. John presumably hoped would be understood
—then why are they so obscure?

If I do not understand the meaning of what I read, how can I
respond to the teachings of Christianity?

If I happen to begin at this point, right at the outset of my quest
I am baffled.

But then, come to think of it, how do I understand anything?

*

Understand . . . a word in the English language . . . under-stand.
To stand under.

I under-stand some thing, some idea, some concept . . .

I comprehend or perceive the meaning of . . .

I mentally recognize and grasp the significance, or explanation,
or cause, or nature of . . .

I know how to deal with . . .

How do I come to under-stand something?

What do I require in order that I can under-stand something?

Is it necessary that I should learn everything about something
before I am able to under-stand it?

Why should it be that someone can apparently understand
something when I cannot? What do they have that I do not?

Where does understanding take place?

In *mind*.

*

As we travel in space and time from place to place and from day
to day, how closely and deeply do we observe the processes that go
on in the mind?

Let us take an example.

You are reading this page. What is going on?

In order to be able to read, you first have to learn to read.

To begin with, certainly with effort on your part, you learn to
associate the shape of a letter with the sound that it represents, a
sound that you have already heard and memorized. Then you put

several letters together and form a simple word—a "sound-shape". The word that you form, if it is, say, a noun, is a representation or symbol of the object that it applies to—its name-sound in visual form.

Thus CAT immediately summons to the reader's mind the image of a small, furry animal—and so distinct is the symbol CAT that the reader knows immediately that it does not stand for a dog or a rabbit. The reader immediately under-stands what the word stands for.

However, the process only takes place if I have already seen, experienced and learnt about the existence of small feline creatures and if I have already learnt and memorized that they are called by the name CAT.

If I am not, say, an expert zoologist, it is unlikely that reading the two words MACACA FUSCATA will call into my mind the image of a Japanese Snow Monkey. MACACA FUSCATA is a meaningless jumble of letters. I may be able to translate the letters into sounds— and with those sounds may be able to pronounce the words correctly; but the words are as nothing to me until I have learnt to associate them with knowledge and experience.

*

Does that mean then that the words of St. John are meaningless to me because I lack certain knowledge and experience?

If I read the word GOD, what happens? What does the word call into my mind? Does it invoke anything really meaningful?

Perhaps we should see that religious scriptures are human attempts to describe experience and do not in themselves prove anything?

Perhaps we should accept that we cannot take "someone else's word" for absolute, factual validity?

But maybe those words can somehow inform, illuminate, give meaning to, confirm *our own experience*?

Yes, we may first have to become familiar with the scriptures as a first step—just as we once had to learn to read. But such learning will be impotent until the words come to have meaning through being associated with experience.

The Word is an abstract concept—until it has been heard.

*

It would seem therefore that words in themselves are a form of communication that has certain limits in that they depend on the limit of experience of the speaker or writer and of the listener or reader. They give "in-form-ation"; but their interpretation will depend on the association in mind of those who are using them.

We continuously depend upon words to put across personal ideas and requirements in the hope that others will understand what we are trying to convey. In the everyday commerce of ordinary life, it works well enough for those who speak the same language. But in more subtle and abstract matters—such as the meaning of religion— it is extremely difficult and subject to frequent misunderstanding.

However, we must have a certain confidence in the worth of discussing such matters and faith in the search for understanding— otherwise there would now be little point in writing another word on this page!

In so many words, it is often said in the great philosophical and religious traditions—you cannot tell another the Truth; but you can work with another to remove the untruth; and when all the untruth is removed, the Truth is self-evident.

*

Of course, in the process of understanding suggested above, there are important factors that have been omitted.

The most essential is surely that the person reading the words on this page must first have had the *ability* to read long before starting the process of actually learning to read. In fact, it is first necessary to be capable of *listening* (and memorizing, recognizing and associating).

Likewise, before speaking, there must be the ability to translate thought into the spoken word.

First, I hear and memorize the *sounds* peculiar to the language of the country in which I live. These sounds, I discover, placed in

16

certain orders—and moulded by mouth cavity, tongue, teeth and lips—form words and these words are used to represent all forms in the physical world.

Everything in experience, as required, is given an appropriate and representative word.

The first words that we use are nearly all representative of forms in our immediate world— "Mama", "Dada", "Mummy", "Daddy", "baby", "cat", "dog" . . . a rapidly increasing vocabulary of image description, each with an associated experience for the infant who uses them.

Gradually, as we grow in ability and experience, words emerge that not only refer to the physical world but to the subtler experiences of feelings and emotions—hunger, happiness, discomfort, liking, wanting, disliking, gratitude . . .

Simple sentences are formed according to the laws and structure of the particular language—the grammar, syntax, relationship of words to each other and so on.

"I run fast" and "I ran fast"—they mean something different although only one small sound change exists between the two sentences (and only one letter changes in the written script).

"I read fast" and "I read fast"—they are the same written down but I can pronounce "read" in two ways so that one indicates the present and the other the past. We can imagine how easily mistakes can be made translating from one language into another. ("And the light shineth in darkness"—present tense; "and the darkness comprehended it not"—past tense. Deliberate or not?)

But, it is not our intention here to go into the complicated science of etymology nor to study and analyse the phenomenon we call language. Let us simply acknowledge that, given the gifts of listening and speaking, writing and reading, we take much for granted and make do with a great deal of approximation. The communicating of anything at all subtle and abstract is not as straightforward and foolproof as we often assume.

Language is the result of a lifetime's practice and adaptation. This is true both for the individual person and for the "universal" person—mankind. It is language that has given man his dominant status in nature.

On the other hand, he has evolved many different languages. One has only to cross an entirely arbitrary, imaginary line, a frontier, to find that one cannot understand nor be understood. This gives rise to one of man's most persistent and inhibiting problems—misunderstanding, between one individual and another, between one nation and another.

And it does mean that we have to be circumspect in our exploration of the old scriptures. There has to be a limit to the experience and therefore the understanding of the chroniclers, of the later interpreters, the translators and the expounders. Again, there can only be validity in those scriptures if they in some way illuminate our own experience, no matter at what level it takes place.

*

And we must not be confined just to interpretation of words.

Behind each language—coming before each language—there is *sound*.

There are vocal sounds common to all people, no matter how they are moulded and expressed by millions of mouths.

And then there is the man-made sound which by-passes the complexities of the spoken word—the sound of song and music.

And then there is the sound of other human emotions—laughter, crying and so on—which is common to all men (and, as always, such sound *means* something, always communicates information).

In nature—and which of us is not in, and of, nature?—we are contained in sound. All kinds of sound continually give us our sense of location—our sense of space and where we are in it.

The running water of a brook does not sound different depending on the language you use; nor the wind passing through the branches of a tree; nor waves crashing against rocks, nor birdsong, nor the bleat of a lamb, nor the buzz of a fly . . . Always sound, always communicating to us.

Is it ever possible, one wonders, to be in an entirely silent place? The deepest silence still seems to have its sound.

If, as an experiment, a human being is placed in a sound-proof cell, whilst he is alive and awake, he will still experience sound. A body is full of sound—breathing, heart beat, blood coursing; even, perhaps, the "sound" of thoughts in the head. The "hum" of silence.

*

We could make a strong case for suggesting that, of all the senses, that of listening most influences the subtle nature of man. It could further be suggested that it is the very sounds we are subjected to constantly throughout our lives, whether we are aware of them or not, that shape our natures.

For sound carries much more than factual information. All sound vibrations affect us, whether harmonious or discordant, whether crude or subtle, forceful or gentle. If I am frequently subjected to harsh sound, my whole being is discomforted, and I have to be strong to withstand it. If I am surrounded by pleasing and calming sound, my whole being—physical and mental—is soothed and pacified.

Have I not understood this in my experience—when I have listened to the gentle sounds of a summer landscape, been disturbed by the sound of violence, lulled by the murmur of a river, been cut by a cry of pain, uplifted by birdsong after winter, jarred by loud machines, moved by strains of music . . . ?

Whatever the quality of the sound, it seems to penetrate and be absorbed in my substance. It sounds within me.

When I really listen to sound, what happens to *me*?

It is as if I become the sound; as if there is only the sound.

*

In the beginning was the Word, and the Word was with God, and the Word was God.

*

Why, in a book about religion, should we give so much attention to words and sound?

19

Partly because all scriptures are written language and because all religious practice places considerable emphasis on the effect and power of sound—the rhythm and pitch of the human voice in the intoning of prayer and chant, the singing and playing of special forms of song and music, the sound quality of the holy place (conducive to contemplation, meditation, silent prayer). The effects on the "being" are strongly emotional—calming, soothing, exhilarating, inspiring—contributory to a mutual communicating or communing through sound and "silence".

The participant, who may come full of mental and physical tension and disturbance, ideally experiences comfort, security, recuperation, revival of strength—and may understand more deeply.

But the degree of his benefit will depend on his listening and understanding at the time. And also the degree and quality of understanding of the priest conducting the service.

*

Let us for a moment consider the act of listening.

Let us try a practical experiment.

First of all, sit comfortably.

Close your eyes, so that you are not distracted by the visual images around you.

Now, be aware.

Feel the weight of your body on the chair.

You will find the mind full of thoughts and "closed in".

How to stop those thoughts?

Just *listen*!

Let the hearing expand into space.

First you will hear the nearest sounds—the loudest and most obvious.

Then your attention—the "focus" of your hearing—can move. You may hear your own breathing, or swallowing, or heart beat.

Then you can move beyond the near sounds.

Really listen.

Far away in the distance . . . the hum of a city, the wind in the trees, the sound of a plane, maybe the hiss of the sea . . . it will depend on where you are.

Keep listening . . .

Are there sounds beyond?

Are there sounds within the sounds?

And beyond the furthest sound? Is there unlimited depth, unlimited height, unlimited space—containing all the sound?

Where are you?

Everywhere?

Who are you?

Nobody?

What can I say?

I am.

Jesus said: *Who has ears to hear, let him hear* . . .

*

The problem with a book is that you cannot do practical things and keep reading at the same time!

So, unless there is someone who can read the above passage to you, it will be impossible to perform the exercise. On the other hand, having read the passage carefully, and having *understood* the idea contained in it, you could now put the book aside and try it.

Why interrupt the reading of these pages with an exercise? To demonstrate that knowledge in theory is a quantum jump from realizing it and understanding it in experience.

*

In the modern world of considerable mental and physical activity directed to the pursuit of one desired objective after another we tend to pay little attention to the subtler information coming through our senses. We seem to be content to live on the "surface" of things. Above all, we rarely stop to listen—to the subtle information of the sounds around us, especially when listening to speech. We tend to overlook what people are *really* saying beneath the superficial meaning of their words; and we rarely listen to what we are *really* saying ourselves. We often do not realize that we do not fully understand the meaning of the words we are using.

*

(Jesus said:) *For by thy words thou shalt be justified, and by thy words thou shalt be condemned.*

(Matthew, 12:37)

*

Religious teachings—and theoretical debates and controversies about theological matters—are utterly idle and useless, if they are not tested and supported in practice and are conducted by men who are not speaking from experience.

I will never find *the* answer through the Christ story—a one, absolute, definitive, all-embracing, perfect answer to satisfy all men; but I may find myself answering to the story as the mind begins to understand it.

*

As we approach the Christ story, we find that we are exhorted to *hear* and to *know what is within our sight.*

Far from there being any suggestion that the Christian message will be full of enigmatic, incomprehensible statements—a kind of divine riddle that we have to work out—it seems that we only have to *look* and *listen* for there to be the possibility of complete understanding—of experiencing the Word.

But is it possible for us to approach something so simply, without an obscuring filter of preconceived ideas and a barrier of pre-conditioning; without opinions and beliefs either in favour of the thing or against it? Can we unravel and abandon our conditioning?

Could we cope with something entirely new—quite beyond the present realms of our imagination, beyond our wildest dreams; a vision so unfamiliar to us that we did not even know the words to describe it?

*

The society into which the man named Jesus was born was already a traditionally religious one.

He was not speaking to a people who had no conception of religious meaning—far from it. They had behind them a long tradition of monotheism. They acknowledged the one, all-seeing, all-knowing, "jealous" god who would allow no compromise and who demanded an undivided, unswerving dedication from man. He was a god who spoke to chosen men down the centuries, giving them his laws and commandments and the rigid regimes of conduct that would "save" them—what foods should and should not be eaten, what sacrifices should be made, what ceremonies should be observed . . .

These people were called Jews and their holy men had for generations prophesied that their god would send a man who would be recognized as a saviour for mankind. He would be born into the world and would speak directly to the people.

But how were they to recognize him?

How could they be sure that a particular man was the one they were waiting for?

Presumably such a man would confirm all that they already knew?

Such a man would surely verify in every detail their long tradition of practice and faith? Otherwise all their efforts would prove to have been a mockery and in vain?

There were some who claimed that the man Jesus was this Messiah.

*

The complexities of the debate as to why the majority of the Jewish people rejected Jesus—and are still to this day awaiting the coming of the "real" Messiah—cannot be entered into here. That must come later when we turn our attention to the Judaic faith-religion.

For now, let us remember that the man Jesus, himself born a Jew, lived within a society which had an established religious form and structure, one that would have claimed true belief and who already worshipped the one god.

If the Messiah were born today, how would he be recognized, who would recognize him, and how would the dignitaries of the established religions react if he told them that they had got it all wrong?

*

As we approach the Christ story and endeavour through the records of his followers to understand the words and deeds of Jesus, we will find the Christ-idea strangely ambivalent. For we will find that devout and intelligent Christians worship Jesus Christ as both an historical figure and as a contemporary divine being.

This gives rise to three possibilities.

Either he was a very special being, in man-form, different from you and me.

Or he was an ordinary human being like you and me, but with a special knowledge and understanding which enabled him to speak and act as we do not. In which case, it is possible that we have the same potential knowledge and understanding within us.

In the latter case, we do no harm in thinking of him as a physical, historical figure.

In the former case, we may consider the possibility that, being "divine" (whatever that may be), "he", spoken of in man-form, need not be thought of as subject to the physical laws of space and time. "He" could be then and always, an eternal principle in form, here and now, in you and me.

Or, the third possibility, *both* cases have validity.

He physically was *and* divinely is.

*

Jesus said unto them, Verily, verily, I say unto you, Before Abraham was, I am.

(John, 8:58)

*

Must we then, from the beginning, accept the "divine", the god-idea?

24

Will it be impossible to take another step into the Christian labyrinth without "believing" certain "incredible" concepts?

No, I do not think so—not necessarily. But we must at the same time be prepared to surrender entirely our preconceptions and our "logical" way of thinking.

We need not believe in the god-idea (and might that not be a relief!); on the other hand, we should not deny the god-idea either. We should not cling to what we think is believable or not believable. We are not setting out to prove that there is a god; we are setting out to see what it may mean to believe—"*in* God".

If we approach with an open mind, neither accepting nor rejecting anything until it has been tried and tested and really listened to—by each one of us on behalf of himself or herself—then, perhaps, we will have "ears to hear".

*

If we admit the possibility that the Christ message could *enlighten* us, if we accept that what was written about Jesus could *enlighten* us, then our minds are open to the possibility of enlightenment. We may discover the Christ through the message.

If Jesus was "god-made-man", and we are "god-made-man", then perhaps the only difference between us is that *he knew it* and *we do not*.

And the light shineth in darkness; and the darkness comprehended it not.

*

The concept of "god in all things"—
All things were made by him; and without him was not anything made that was made—
is the pivotal point of the Christian tradition.

The threefold aspect of God is known as the Trinity: the Father, the Son, the Holy Ghost (or Spirit).

These three aspects are in all things—the Word, the Light, the Life, Christ, my friends, my enemies, work, beauty, ugliness, life, death, birth, joy, suffering . . .

If God made all things, there is not anything, including you and me, which is not from Him, by Him, in Him, of Him . . .

So, how does it come about that, despite such explicit statement, people come to think of God as being *apart* from them?

*

The Trinity—known as the Three Persons of the Trinity.

Person, from the Latin *per-sonare*, "through-*sound*".

A sound, having been made, must be heard for it to be known to exist.

In any exchange of energy, there must always be a trinity of factors—the active, the passive, and the condition for the transmission to take place.

If a word is to be made manifest, there must be a speaker who knows the word and desires to speak it, a listener to hear it, and a medium to carry the vibration-message.

*

How could God know Himself to exist?

*

If Jesus, known as the Christ, was born into this world to manifest "god-made-man" and there is the possibility of my realizing it, then at first sight there are an awful lot of complicated anomalies in the simple comparison of his life and my own—even in the bare outline of his story as told in our first chapter. From a virgin birth right through to being dead and then alive again is a long, long way from my own understanding of the strange enigma that I call my life.

Why, I wonder, does the story seem so alien, so complicated, so mysterious, so incredible?

Is it like trying to understand an entirely foreign language—even worse, possibly written in code? Or like trying to comprehend some totally new object, perhaps one that does not even seem to belong to this planet?

So far as I am concerned, one thing is probable—that if it gets too complicated, I will give up the struggle! Life is difficult enough without my having to try to pit my wits against obscure stories originating two thousand years ago.

Yet . . . I am seeking something—otherwise I would not have embarked on an exploration of the Christ mystery. Something nags me to investigate. What nags me, I wonder? And, honestly, I would not expect to find it easy, would I? If it were easy, the place would be teeming with enlightened people.

A believer might tell me that I am seeking "the kingdom of heaven".

Am I? I don't know.

So, here I am, rather confused, probably ignorant, hopefully innocent, wondering what step to take next.

Perhaps there is no point more appropriate to start than with birth—and, in particular, with that mysterious "virgin birth" which is where the Christian faith-religion began centuries ago.

*

This has been a chapter leading us where?

Why do we think that there is somewhere to go?

We usually think of being led "forwards"; but it is also possible to be led "backwards"!

*

And Jesus called a little child unto him, and set him in the midst of them,

And said, Verily I say unto you, Except ye be converted, and become as little children, ye shall not enter into the kingdom of heaven.

Whosoever therefore shall humble himself as this little child, the same is greatest in the kingdom of heaven.

(Matthew, 18:2–4)

27

Three

How did the Jesus story originate? As we look at the historical records, how did Jesus first appear?

St. Mark simply states that "Jesus came from Nazareth . . . " St. John merely records that one day John the Baptist "seeth Jesus coming unto him . . . " St. Matthew traces the genealogical line from Abraham (three times fourteen generations) and states baldly that his mother "was found with child of the Holy Ghost".

(What, one wonders, is the point of tracing the male line in such detail when, at the final link, Joseph is not the "father" of Jesus?)

It is left to one account only, that of St. Luke, the physician, to give any detail of the conception and birth of Jesus.

(Who, one wonders, told him of the intimate and miraculous events?)

*

And in the sixth month the angel Gabriel was sent from God unto a city of Galilee, named Nazareth,

To a virgin espoused to a man whose name was Joseph, of the house of David; and the virgin's name was Mary.

And the angel came in unto her, and said, Hail, thou that art highly favoured, the Lord is with thee: blessed art thou among women.

And when she saw him, she was troubled at his saying, and cast in her mind what manner of salvation this should be.

And the angel said unto her, Fear not, Mary: for thou hast found favour with God.

And, behold, thou shalt conceive in thy womb, and bring forth a son, and shalt call his name JESUS.

He shall be great, and shall be called the Son of the Highest: and the Lord God shall give unto him the throne of his father David:

And he shall reign over the house of Jacob for ever; and of his kingdom there shall be no end.

Then said Mary unto the angel, How shall this be, seeing I know not a man?

And the angel answered and said unto her, The Holy Ghost shall come upon thee, and the power of the Highest shall overshadow thee: therefore also that holy thing which shall be born of thee shall be called the Son of God.

(Luke, 1:26–35)

*

It is, indeed, a strange story.

We cannot know much about how it was appreciated by minds over past centuries; but it is particularly strange for we of the scientific age who read it today.

If we take it literally, it is full of incomprehensibilities. And the danger is that as we endeavour to reconcile it with modern knowledge, to make it palatable to our logical minds—as we try to translate it into *our terms*—we may "water it down", lose the essence of it by misinterpreting the words and thus dissipate the significance of what is being told.

Unless, of course, we are wasting our time because the whole Christ story was and is an elaborate hoax.

But does that seem likely?

We have written evidence that the stories concerning the man called Jesus have been around for centuries. They must have stemmed from somewhere; there must have been an originator, or originators, of them. Is it likely that this person, or persons, decided to tell an intricate, imaginative and fantastic fiction simply to deceive or entertain people? Someone wanted someone to understand something, surely?

If it were either a deliberate deception or a harmless tale, does it not seem extraordinary that so many intelligent people over the centuries have revered it and given it credence?

*

29

But then, the whole nature of truth and untruth is called into account. Did the person, or persons, who first decreed and believed that the earth was flat lie and deceive? They actually *believed* that it was so. Then surely they were not lying? It is simply that we would say now that their belief was mistaken. But the point is, it was the truth for them.

So, before we become too confident, where do we stand in our belief? Ought we not to allow that maybe our beliefs are mistaken—that maybe "truth" can change for us also?

The world, we now say, is round (or nearly so). We think we have ample evidence to confirm this model as absolute fact. But a few years ago, man set foot on the moon. It is now a possibility that future generations could colonize the moon, making it an "island" or extension of the earth. Perhaps people will then speak of the earth *and* the moon as "the world". At that time, the world would cease to be "round"; it would become . . . "egg-shaped". Would not the inhabitants of that egg-shaped world consider us limited and mistaken in our limited outlook and say that the "truth" we believed was only relative to our time?

All speculation . . . but perhaps it may serve to make us question the nature of what we call "truth" and demonstrate that belief is temporary, fashionable and relative—not absolute.

*

Can you say honestly that anything is the truth, the whole truth and nothing but the truth?

"The truth of the world" is what you *believe* it to be—until it is "proved" otherwise and then your belief changes.

*

Let us therefore in considering the Christ story not worry as to the motives of the story tellers. Let us assume that they believed what they were talking about. And that those who relate the story today also believe and that therefore it is the truth for them within the limits of their understanding. (For what man would claim to have complete and unlimited understanding?)

30

The "believers" may not, in the end, convince *me* that there is any value in their beliefs for *me*—but that should in no way detract from the value of their belief for them. My opinion as to the validity of their beliefs is bound to be related to the limits of *my* understanding.

We have already said—and must keep reminding ourselves—that the great disservice of believers is that they should feel compelled to impose their beliefs on others. (Strength of belief has much to do with the acquisition of power and hence the ability of one man to exercise dominance over another.) But also, let us not fall into the equally dangerous presumption of feeling free to attack other men's belief, simply because we cannot understand it, or are jealous of it.

Let us be particularly wary if we have nothing to offer in exchange. It is far easier to be destructive than constructive. And if we do have something to offer, and it is unacceptable to another, then let us leave it at that. The world, it seems, is plagued by people who think they know what is best for other people.

*

Jesus instructed his disciples to "spread the good news"; he did not say "*persuade* them to believe it".

*

Finally, and most important even if rather obvious, if I am truly searching for the answers to the deepest questions and have decided to explore the Christ story in the hope that through it I will find the answers—then I must allow that the teachings have a validity, at least for as long as I am pursuing that path into the labyrinth.

Let me put aside, for the moment, all suggestions that the whole story could be a hoax, or a pack of lies, or a merely entertaining tale. Let me acknowledge that nearly two thousand years ago a group of people were inspired by a man's words and example, and believed in him and his teaching with such conviction and passion that their "sound" has echoed through generation after generation right through to today.

*

Of course, the "sound" will have been subject to such modifications as any process of transmission must be. It may have been a little like the party game:

A group of players stand in a line. The first person whispers a message to the person standing next to him and he, in turn, whispers the message he believes he has heard to the person standing next to him . . . and so on, down the line. Finally, the message reaches the last person—who speaks out loud his version of the message. The result can be very amusing. The original message—and especially the emphasis and tone of it—can have changed beyond recognition, as each person heard and interpreted what he thought his neighbour had whispered to him.

And written messages are even more vulnerable to mistakes in transmission. For example, you may be told that I said "Go away!" to someone. You will understand the meaning of the words—but you will not know whether I was entreating, ordering, reluctant to say it, angry with the other person . . .

What we can say is that if you receive a message, you try to make the best possible *sense* of it.

*

Who has ears to hear, let him hear . . .

We do not know how "accurate" the Christ story is *now*.

But maybe it is a sufficiently faithful record for the "essential sense" to have survived.

It is interesting that we use the word "sense"—to make sense.

Which of the senses do we use to "make sense"?

Each, or all, of them, depending on the circumstance.

In the light, you make sense of an object by seeing it. In the dark, you do it by touching and feeling it.

You make sense of a perfume by smelling it.

You make sense of a flavour by tasting it.

You make sense of a sound by hearing and listening to it.

And if you cannot make sense of something, you may call it "nonsense".

The senses are not however immediately reliable—or, more accurately, interpretation of sensory information can be confusing. Have you ever been given a cup of coffee when you *believed* it to be tea? It does not taste like tea—or, persuaded that it is tea, then it is disgusting tea! But you did not immediately recognize it as coffee. What happened to the sense of taste? It was confused by a preconceived idea; it was not given what it had been "programmed" to expect.

Maybe then, "coming to our senses" may have something to do with removing the confusion of preconception and prejudice from our minds?

Belief pre-disposes the mind to particular and possibly limited interpretation; it may well deny the mind a more "sens-ible" view.

*

So how does the mind make sense of something? What sense is that? Is it not something to do with the "under-standing" we mentioned in the first chapter? Something makes sense if we re-cognize and under-stand it—if it accords with our previous learning and experience.

But how, I wonder, does the mind accept and assimilate an entirely new idea—an idea of which it has no previous concept or experience? May not the mind have its own sense—something to do with "common sense", with reason ("the *sound* of things"), with intuition ("inner sight or knowledge")?

How did we, each one of us, first start to assimilate impressions when we were newly born, when we were "innocent"? By what criteria did we begin to select—to accept and reject?

How do we now, as we consider the Christ story, wipe clean centuries of preconception and prejudice, persuasion and interpretation, about "god" and "religion"? How do we start anew—fresh, unprejudiced, free of assumption, innocent? How do we become "open" again to receive impressions clearly, as though for the first time, "as a little child"? How can we hear a "new testament" now?

By watching and listening.

It must be like learning a new language. You do not really speak a new language naturally and with confidence until you stop *thinking* in your former tongue. You have to stop translating from the old and so absorb the new that you *think* it.

But, what is "thinking"?

Supposing that in equipping our minds to take part in and deal with worldly life, we have built in logical and analytical ways of processing information about the world; we learn to deal with scientific, practical, "provable" facts. At the same time, we may have ignored the possibility that this is an elementary and limited use of the mind and that, when more mature, it may be able to comprehend what may seem illogical and "unscientific"—knowledge which is actually more refined and powerful than "relative fact". In concerning ourselves strictly with the mundane, may we not close our minds to subtler ideas?

Where do "ideas" come from?

How often do we leave room in our minds to "have an idea"?

*

The mind cannot *conceive* ideas at will. They become mentally appreciated when they have become, as it were, "made flesh", cognizable in form, when they become manifest as words and images.

Is not the profound realization of an idea—unconceived by *my* will and yet taking form in the "womb" of *my* mind—what we call "inspiration"?

And do we not usually rely upon "clever people" in our society to come up with the odd inspiration from time to time to set us on a new line of enquiry or development?

The list of inspirations that have changed the course of history is long. Many have been apparently useful and many have been apparently detrimental—yet all of them have got us to where we are now.

From the discovery of the wheel to the splitting of the atom, all such discoveries have come through the ordinary thinking processes

34

of the human mind being inspired by an idea for which there was no precedent in the experience *of the time*.

At the moment of inspiration—like a split-second entry of some "spirit"—what was inconceivable is transformed into knowledge and experience. It becomes a manifest reality in the world.

However, it is usually the case that the individual who is inspired has been querying, applying his thinking and imagination, making efforts to "align" himself, perhaps unknowingly, with the possibility of particular inspiration *before* the "new" idea actually comes to him. The idea meets a mind prepared to realize the potential.

For example, whoever "thought *up*" the wheel was probably sick and tired of dragging along heavy burdens. He required an alternative. Only when he required the alternative did he unknowingly prepare himself and align himself with the possibility of recognizing the potential "wheel".

But what about that inspirational idea? It must have "come from somewhere". Was it the inevitable result of a logical chain of events —that, maybe, is how the ordinary mind would see it? Or was the wheel, say, waiting to be discovered by someone sooner or later? You might say that it already existed in the future? The ordinary mind may find that difficult to comprehend, and yet . . . Either way, it was "born" when it was required. But, still, where did it come from?

The word "inspire" means, literally, "to breathe or blow into" and is related to the word "spirit". It serves very well, as "well-made" words can, to describe the impregnation of the prepared and "innocent" mind by a powerful idea.

So where is the source of the "breath"; where does it "blow" from?

*

These questions and considerations could be significant when we turn to explore the message of the "virgin" conception and birth in the Christ story.

For the first great problem we have to face is that we appear to be asked to believe that a child was born in an abnormal way—from the scientific point of view, in a way utterly contrary to the proven laws of genetics.

However, how does our acceptance of the factual information that the sperm fertilizes the ovum, that the male chromosomes pair off with their complementary female opposites, and that the embryo then grows in the womb relate to the question:

"Where did *I* come from?"

It may be biologically indisputable that it is through the coupling of the male and female that a third body is originated, but is that the *entire* story of my creation?

In all honesty, what has the copulation of my parents to do with *me* now?

Conversely, when my mother and father copulated, had they any conception who or what they were creating?

Who gave birth to *who*, and by *whose* will?

*

Can any two human beings—one male and the other female—profoundly understand what is going on when they think they "decide to have a baby"? By their act, they cannot guarantee that conception will take place, they cannot determine the number or sex of their offspring. And the sex of the new being is only one of the numerous characteristics that will start to define that third individual and make him or her different from all others.

There will be inherited similarities, of course. In physical appearance, a child may bear striking resemblances to one or other of the parents, or to both of them. But the physical attributes are only the "wrapping" as it were. It is the particular characteristics of the mind—what takes place in it—which gradually sets that being apart as an individual person.

Certainly a child will acquire some mental characteristics from the parents during the early, formative years; and these may persist for the rest of the person's life (and he will benefit with some and suffer with others). But are there not more fundamental features—

36

talents, flaws, dispositions—which distinguish the child from both parents? Where do they come from?

There will be no simple answers to such questions—and it is not appropriate to pursue them here—but, what is certain is that no parents can decide what their child is going to be like.

*

Finally, there is the "life" of the child.

What has the fertilization of a minute ovum by an even more minute sperm, and the gestation in the womb, got to do with the "breathing of life into" *me* at birth?

What is "life" anyway?

Here we stand supremely innocent and ignorant.

We say "we live" and yet we do not know what "life" *is*, where it "comes from" nor "where it goes" at death. I say "my life" and yet do I *have* it; do I by my will "take it up"? Can I by my will "keep" it? If I kill myself, what have I done with it?

Of all the absurd beliefs that a man may hold, surely none could be more so than that inherent in the claim that he possesses his life?

For all his vast learning, man has not as yet been able to create life, even in so small a thing as a single blade of grass.

I assume that my body was formed inside my mother as the result of impregnation by my father; but are they the mother and father of that essential core of my being, that "I" who is here and now?

*

In view of so much ignorance about so many fundamental things, would it be presumptuous to suggest that every newly created being is an "inspiration", is "breathed into" by mysterious "spirit"?

Whose inspiration am I?

Would it be presumptuous to say that every conception is "innocent", "unknown" by man, in "darkness"; and that every birth is a unique, miraculous, "virgin" creation, in which mankind is the substance and the instrument. The process takes place without his will; he can do no more than *be prepared* to accept it and realize it for what it is.

37

*

Then said Mary unto the angel, How shall this be, seeing I know not a man?

*

Could it be that really we are considering not only a possibly literal story but *also* a *symbolic* story—one that is intimately to do with you and me *now* as we wonder at the mystery of our existing?

*

. . . therefore also that holy thing which shall be born of thee . . .

*

If the story is fact—if the man Jesus *was* born of a virgin without copulation having taken place—then here would be such a mystery and such a magic that, being *proved*, I would certainly want to hear and know everything there was to be heard and known about such a man. I would be absorbed—perhaps awed and inspired—by the challenge to my mind.

However, apart from capturing my attention and making me avidly curious, would it really alter very much *for me*? It would still depend on what the man *did* and *said* whether he could influence my life or not.

If I am not impressed by him, then the most that he can expect, so far as I am concerned, is that I will think him a freak of nature and add him to my list of inexplicable phenomena.

For, if I do not *understand* something, I will eventually cease to consider it. Such is the nature of my mind that I will not for ever keep trying to fathom something that I have decided is beyond me; I prefer to put it aside and get on with something more tangible and rewarding.

Am I alone in this I wonder?

There is one other alternative. I could ignore the fact that the story makes no sense to my intellect and simply decide to believe it, with all my heart.

(But if I am able to do that, at least I ought to look at the motive. The heart is notorious for undertaking foolish commitments!)

*

But, if the story is symbolic of something that I do not at the moment comprehend intellectually, I must take note of what my heart "feels" about it. For the "heart" has this strange "intuition" which will not be gainsaid. The heart will not let the intellect rest if it is not satisfied.

Do we not sometimes "feel" something to be right or wrong, even though that feeling may contradict the intellect?

And do we not mean by that that we "sense" the truth or untruth without necessarily being able to bring forward any evidence to prove it?

Spirituality tends to be deadened by the intellectualizing of the head alone; and it tends to be deadened by the "blind" faith of the heart alone. But if head and heart work together . . . then, for example, the symbolism of religion may spring to life . . .

*

Let us go a little further in touching on the possibility of the Christ story being symbolic.

Mary, in her innocence, is told by an "angel" that she will bear a child and that the child will be sent from "God".

What is an "angel"?

Let us dispense immediately with the evanescent, hermaphrodite images that are supposed to fly about with wings protruding from their backs—images which are familiar to anyone who is acquainted with the religious paintings or the illuminated texts or the stained glass works executed by artists of the Christian tradition. For we should recognize that all "art" is artefact—something interpreted and expressed in human workmanship, possibly inspired but none the less interpretative. And, especially in the religious context, the artist is faced with the problem of representing images of "unknown form"; at best he can only do it *symbolically* and what may be an appropriate symbol at one time may not be so at another.

An "angel" is literally a "messenger". Where do ideas come from? How do they manifest to us? As messages?

39

And the angel came in unto her, and said, Hail, thou that art highly favoured, the Lord is with thee: blessed art thou among women.

Could not—should not—a sense of being honoured as a vehicle for the creation of a new being enter into and be appreciated by any woman who contemplates her ability to be a mother?

*

Mary was "a virgin espoused to a man". "Espoused" means to give or to take in marriage or betrothal. And both of these conditions essentially imply "being true to word or vow given to someone".

Mary was, in today's vernacular, engaged to be married: but she asks, when told she is to have a baby, "How shall this be, seeing I know not a man?"

This seems a pretty unequivocal statement.

On the face of it, she certainly "knew a man" in the sense that she was acquainted with one, namely Joseph.

Some would maintain that the expression is a euphemistic way of saying that she had not had sexual intercourse with a man. Fair enough if she was still a virgin and was not yet married. But why should she ask the question, for the angel said "thou shalt", implying the future, and she knew she was going to marry Joseph? What reason would she have to suppose that the angel did not mean a child by him?

It is pointless to debate and speculate about such literal semantics. Whatever else the expression may be intended to convey, could it not symbolically convey the doubt of any mind in humility: "I am not prepared, do not have the knowledge, to be able to receive the Christ message"?

*

Even if we take the ordinary sense in which we would use the word "know", we should not confine it to the superficial connotation of "being acquainted with".

Will any woman ever "know" a man; will any man ever "know" a woman?

"To know" is commonly used to cover several, subtly different mental experiences—cognize, recognize, identify, be assured of, be acquainted with, be informed of, be aware of, be versed in, to have knowledge of . . .

You and I may be informed *about* each other, be acquainted *with* each other, be aware *of* each other and we may recognize and identify each other *by* our characteristics when we next meet. But we cannot *be* each other—not ever.

Even if we know everything *about* each other, if we cannot *be* each other, the one cannot truly *know* the other.

*

We can know *about* the sperm fertilizing the ovum—but we cannot know it happening. We can only be in ignorance at the miraculous moment of conception.

Mary was a "virgin" and "did not know a man" at the moment of conception in that she was innocent of what was happening inside her—just as the mind is unaware of an idea's approach and entry. She was "inspired"—as every mother is—to be the instrument through which every divine being is born. She was, and is, as "eternal mothering", the medium through which the "Holy Ghost", derived from the eternal "Father", enters every "Son".

What more perfect symbol do we need to indicate the principals involved in the giving of life, the entry of spirit into matter?

Does it help my mind understand the factors comprising "my" life?

The mind may not "know" the principals—but it can acknowledge and witness the miracle of their inter-play and realize its utter dependence on "inspiration"—even if it is, understandably, reluctant to have to give a name to the source of that inspiration. Once cleared of presumption and realizing its role, then it may experience true humility and be in a condition capable of prayer and praise.

*

Where did "I" come from?
Who am "I"?

41

. . . therefore also that holy thing which shall be born of thee shall be called the Son of God.

*

The "father" role in this complex story is revealing. So significant is the symbol that in the Christian terminology the word is used as a synonym for the principal "God".

How was Joseph—the one who had given his word to Mary—faring while his espoused was growing "great with child"—a child whom he had to admit was not his own?

In St. Matthew's Gospel, we may read as follows:

Now the birth of Jesus Christ was on this wise: When as his mother Mary was espoused to Joseph, before they came together, she was found with child of the Holy Ghost.

Then Joseph her husband, being a just man, and not willing to make her a publick example, was minded to put her away privily.

But while he thought on these things, behold, the angel of the Lord appeared unto him in a dream, saying, Joseph, thou son of David, fear not to take unto thee Mary thy wife: for that which is conceived in her is of the Holy Ghost.

And she shall bring forth a son, and thou shalt call his name JESUS: for he shall save his people from their sins.

Now all this was done, that it might be fulfilled which was spoken of the Lord by the prophet, saying,

Behold, a virgin shall be with child, and shall bring forth a son, and they shall call his name Emmanuel, which being interpreted is, God with us.

Then Joseph being raised from sleep did as the angel of the Lord had bidden him, and took unto him his wife:

And knew her not till she had brought forth her firstborn son: and he called his name JESUS.

(Matthew, 1:18–25)

When did you first realize that you existed? When did you awake from the dream of your childhood and say "I am"?

*

42

Taken at its literal level, this aspect of the Mary and Joseph story makes one wonder. They appear to have been wonderful parents. For neither of them, in the reported circumstances, would ever have claimed the child as their own, of their own making. He was "Emmanuel, which being interpreted is, God with us."

What a deal of misunderstanding could be averted if all parents saw so clearly and objectively the nature of their roles! It is little wonder that Jesus and his parents should be known as "The Holy Family".

Mary and Joseph may or may not have comprehended what was going on—but they do appear to have accepted it and not allowed any preconceived beliefs as to who possessed what to get in the way of their real responsibility.

*

So, the Son of God is born.

And it came to pass in those days, that there went out a decree from Caesar Augustus, that all the world should be taxed.

(Luke, 2:1)

They seem to have been familiar hard times!

The world then was the "known world", the Roman Empire. Now we know there were other worlds—India, China . . . But then the Roman Empire was "the world" for the purpose of our story tellers.

To be "taxed" means to register or enrol for fiscal purposes (the "public treasury or revenue"); to burden, to accuse or censure; to assess; to examine (accounts) in order to allow or disallow items . . .

In other words, "the world" was being questioned as to the earning and spending of its resources, was being asked to account for itself.

And, if the world, then each person in it was being required to demonstrate their worth, whether they were earning their living and paying their dues.

And is that not when we have suggested that "inspiration" is likely to occur? When man cannot get any further along his selected

43

way on the basis of his present methods, then he calls himself to account and looks for "inspiration" because his mode of living is falling short of his expectations—and the world demands that he should prove his worth.

*

But is inspiration, when it comes, immediately accepted by the world at large? Is it not at first often dismissed as being fantasy, foolhardy, far-fetched? It is not "heard" and it might be said of it that it is not admitted.

And she brought forth her first-born son, and wrapped him in swaddling clothes, and laid him in a manger; because there was no room for them in the inn.

(Luke, 2:7)

But if the inspired hold firm to the revelation, it will not be gainsaid. For that inspiration is born and is a reality.

The inspired may keep quiet about their revelation if it meets resistance; but they protect it and nurture it. They allow it to mature and wait until the world is ready to accept it.

When the consciousness of yourself first dawns in your mind, the mind is full of the powers of alien belief; the consciousness remains hidden and is not introduced to the world; it must remain protected until it matures.

*

Does it matter, now, if historically it can be proved that Caesar Augustus did decree at that time that all the world should be taxed?

Does such evidence *really* prove anything about the story?

Any wise story teller will draw on factual background to weave his story; just as he will draw upon local colour and characters that he has experienced in his life; just as he will use analogy and allegory to hint at his message.

Human "life" draws upon the sperm and the ovum to manifest itself. Perhaps even the "creator" relies upon the "creation" to demonstrate "himself" to "himself"?

*

However, with any inspirational idea that matures, there comes a time when it must be announced to the world.

When a child is born into a devout Christian family—or, at least, the family follows the orthodox programme—the first important religious ceremony for that child is the baptism.

At the baptism, the child is ceremonially given his or her Christian name (or names). The child ceases to be a nameless body or being; he or she becomes identifiable by a particular "sound" and is recognized as a certain person. Now the child, once the name is learnt and memorized, may be *called*—by that name.

And common belief is such that people think they "know" the child because they can identify him or her by that name.

*

But, are you just your name?

Are you any more *you* after a name has been given to you?

Do you know yourself by your name?

A name does not tell you who you are—but it gives you response-ability.

*

Is an idea any less valid before it is taken up than after? It is the same idea before and after it is announced. Its validity lies in whether it proves its worth or not.

*

Is this book a book if you, or someone, is not reading it?

It may exist, but if no one knows it exists, can it truly be said that it is a book?

Was a round wooden object something different before someone first called it a "wheel"? Does naming it change it in any way?

Naming enables something to be recognized so that it may be called upon to serve a function, to be responsible for what it is.

Perhaps baptism, as a symbolic act, represents the moment when a sound is given meaning as a word and that word is applied to form so that it may be recognized?

The sounds were presumably there before; the sounds could

45

have made words before; but, until they were given meaning, they could not be spoken and used.

What was "God" before that name was given?

"In the beginning was the Word . . . "; what "word"?

Must we not *know* the meaning of the name "God" before there is any value in speaking it?

Must we not *hear* the Word before we can possibly understand it?

*

Jesus is reported as having been baptized and St. Mark records that "immediately the Spirit driveth him into the wilderness".

A wilderness is a region uncultivated and uninhabited; a pathless or desolate tract of any kind; a part of a garden or estate allowed to run wild . . . the present world . . . from which we obtain the word "bewildered".

*

It sounds as though Jesus experienced the world very much as you and I experience it—a bewildering place.

Perhaps we can also appreciate that entering the "wilderness" is an apt description of any person's experience of entering the labyrinth of the mind—which we may well find "uncultivated", "pathless", "desolate", "running wild".

Perhaps, as soon as he was named and became responsible to others, Jesus was as confused and innocent as we are now—as we endeavour to sense with our minds and hearts the meaning of our being in existence?

*

Because we cannot *know* our own conception, our moment of incarnation, is it fruitful to dwell too long on the "fatherless" conception of the Christian story? Only if it reveals something to us about our present state.

Who am I? Where did I come from? Who are the parents of the essential "I" in me?

Because we are not likely to recall the time when we were first ceremonially named, can we begin to comprehend the meaning of

46

the baptism of Christ? Only if it helps us to comprehend the meaning of our being given an identity.

Why was I called into being? Why do I need to be identified? To whom am I answerable?

*

Whether Jesus existed in fact or not, the story of his life can inspire me if I do not "set him apart" by believing that he was unique and totally different from me; if, in other words, the story of his life and experience somehow links with mine.

This is important. For only someone who has *heard* and *answered* the deep questions that I have heard can possibly give guidance to me in my quest to answer them.

*

There is much to be explored in just the little we have touched upon. Once we begin to recognize and feel response to the possible symbolism, all kinds of paths appear for exploring the mystery of our existence.

At some point, I may find that I am called upon to "believe". But until I am confronted with it and really understand what "believing" is, I should not expect to have to exercise this strange capacity "unknowingly".

Let the final words of this chapter be a "saying" of Jesus from the Gospel according to Thomas. I may not *know* what the words mean intellectually; but perhaps I can recognize the experience of what they convey.

Jesus said: Let him who seeks, not cease seeking until he finds, and when he finds, he will be troubled, and when he has been troubled, he will marvel and he will reign over the All.

(Thomas, Log. 2)

47

Four

When Jesus heard it, he saith unto them, They that are whole have no need of the physician, but they that are sick: I came not to call the righteous, but sinners to repentance.

(Mark, 2:17)

＊

Anyone approaching the Christian faith-religion will sooner or later—and it is likely to be sooner—be confronted with the concept "sin".

Because the concept and belief as to what "sinning" means is so crucial, and can so profoundly influence behaviour in the world, perhaps we should pause here in our exploration of the Christ story to consider what it means.

How do I interpret what I have heard about "being a sinner"?

The dictionary tells me that sin is a moral offence or shortcoming, especially from the point of view of religious conduct; an offence generally; a shame, a pity . . .

＊

To sin, as I understand it, means to do those things that I should not do, and, a little more subtly, to fail to do those things that I should do—the sins of commission and omission.

＊

That, at first, seems pretty straightforward. And, if I obey the rules, I need not worry about it any more.

But who tells me what I should or should not do?

Can I really believe and trust whoever it is, and be certain that they really know what is best for me?

Who has been given this authority and why?

Why should there be things that I am capable of doing—and yet not be allowed to do them?

Why should I be "bound" to do things when I do not want to do them and do not know why I should?

*

It soon becomes clear as I follow this depth of enquiry that judging whether I am a sinner or not is not all that straightforward.

I can see that certain obligations are reasonable and must have come about through necessity. I can imagine that from the time human beings started to live together in communities certain codes and rules of behaviour were bound to emerge. Presumably, primitive man, at some point in his development, found that there were benefits to be gained from living in association with others. Hunting, for example, must have proved more effective if there was more than one man pursuing the prey. If six men hunted an animal, they could encircle and trap it. The chances of success were improved by cooperation.

But the animal having been caught and killed, the meat would have to be divided between the six. So there then arose the whole concept of shared ownership through shared work. "This is my portion; that is your portion."

And if either of us takes more than we are entitled to, that is not fair; it is "stealing". Thus, the benefits of cooperation immediately introduce problems of fairness, sharing, rights of possession, apportionment . . . and so on.

Also, we can imagine that having dismembered the beast, the six would need to compete for the choicest parts; and here would arise all manner of debate over such moral questions as the obligation of the stronger to the weaker.

And so, we may surmise, something had to be done to avoid constant strife. As the communities expanded and became more organized, so laws emerged to ensure the smooth running of life—

49

how to gain maximum benefit from the advantages and eliminate the disadvantages.

(And this has been man's continuing endeavour ever since!)

*

Once communal living is introduced, rules and laws and moral obligations are sure to follow.

However, a law is useless unless it is "under-stood" and obeyed. It is not sufficient simply to agree not to steal—for what you agree today may be forgotten in the heat of the moment tomorrow. The temptation arises inevitably for the individual to give precedence to self-survival over the community's survival; hence the threat of potential anarchy which the majority would maintain must be averted at all costs.

The laws have to be instilled into the members and enforced, in order that they may be known by all to be laws. And for those who break them, there must be retribution.

We can imagine that if a member of a primitive society broke the law a rough and vicious form of punishment would have been meted out to him. Perhaps he was thrown out of the community and left to fend for himself; or he was summarily maimed or executed.

Such retribution may originally have resulted from a consensus of opinion within the tribe; but we may presume that gradually certain men, or one man, assumed leadership over the rest. Perhaps he was the strongest—or the most cunning or intelligent. This man would have become the law-maker, the judge and the punish-ment-giver. Accepted as such, he was invested with power over others.

And thus there is established another problem that has exercised the minds of men ever since. How much power should a man, or a group of men, be allowed to exercise over others? How can the community be protected against the abuse of such power—if the power is used for self-advantage at the expense of the community's advantage.

*

Now, I can see that all such laws come about through need and expediency; and they are "man-made".

As lawful behaviour developed in communities, so came the opportunity for other potential benefits to emerge. A man was no longer alone; he had the opportunity to develop communication with others. He began to develop the potential of language. He must have felt the urge to share his thoughts and questions.

Having perhaps wondered to himself about such things, he could now find words to express the questions which mystified him:

"Where did we come from?"

"What are we?"

"Who am I?"

Yet again, such problematic questions have been with us ever since.

*

Perhaps, one day long ago, one man said to another: "Let's call ourselves 'men'." And perhaps one man once asked his companion: "Who am I?", and the other replied: "You are 'you'!"

For me to say "I am a man" or "I am me and you are you" may be a simple enough answer; but does it go "deep" enough? By such words, things are named and recognized and separated; but is that what they *are*? According to the penetration of my question, so I will look for an answer of adequate "depth".

As we ponder how we arrived at where we are now, we may suggest that, for those men of prehistory, all they had to work on and rely on was the "memory" of the tribe.

Old men told stories of their youth and stories they had been told by other old men, who, in turn, had heard them when they were young from those who were then old . . . and so on. They would have told of the battles, the emigrations, the famines, the hardships, the times of plenty—everything significant and exceptional, including the great leaders there had been and what they had said and done.

Eventually, there would have been established the story of the tribe, a mixture of myth and history, and inevitably, woven into it, the tradition of law and codes of conduct belonging to that tribe.

51

In time, it would become as if the history-mythology had no "beginning"—simply the limit of human memory. And it would be as though the fundamental laws, for the present generation of transitory mortals, were absolute, eternal, sacred and irrefutable. The very first men to establish them would be respected as having been exceptionally wise—perhaps as having exceptional powers?

As the laws became sacred so did the men of long ago who originated them. They were ancestors worthy of remembrance and worship; they would become as "gods".

For the time being, the mythology would serve as an explanation —the answer to the questions.

*

How far we seem from those primitive times!

Clearly, such times can have little to do with me and my experience of the world as it is now.

But is that really a valid assumption?

However sophisticated and advanced our times may be, how did I come to believe what I do? How "deep" are my answers to the eternal questions? Have man's problems essentially changed? How different now are law and religion? Is my "tribal lore" so different?

I have learnt and I have memorized. But how good are the memories of my teachers? How *did* the wisdom of *my* tribe originate?

*

Except ye be converted, and become as little children . . .

*

I can suppose that one flaw must have emerged in the development of law as hypothesized above.

In order that the law could be enforced, there had to be punishment. You feared breaking the law because the consequent punishment would be unpleasant—and the more serious the offence, the more painful the consequences. You had to be made to "suffer" for your misdeed.

But . . . what if you were not found out? What if you found a way of cheating society in a way beneficial to yourself and that you managed it so cunningly that the community could not discover that it was you?

This must have been a tricky one for the leaders of the tribe. Not only was there the fact that someone was managing to avoid justice but there was the danger that if others saw that it was possible they might be tempted to try it also. How to get round that?

Supposing . . . supposing that the revered ancestors were able, even after death, to see and know what was going on? And further, because it was inevitably offensive to them, the founders of the law, then the punishment they could bring upon the offender could be far more awful than anything the tribe could devise?

Well, that might work as a partial deterrent; but then there would be those who committed crime and then waited, no doubt in fear and trembling, for the "wrath to descend" and . . . nothing happened!

So then, one day, some cunning law-maker came up with the trump card.

Supposing . . . supposing that the all-seeing and all-knowing immortals recorded the transgressions and then, adding together the sins of a lifetime, administered terrible punishment *after death*?

I may not believe in the "gods" and I may think that "eternal suffering after death" is a bit far-fetched . . . but can I be absolutely sure? Dare I risk ignoring the warning?

*

At some point in the history of man—emerging from or quite independent of the idea of immortal ancestors—there came the concept of invisible powers which influence life on earth. These powers were "spirits" which could be imagined in human or other recognizable forms. As super-men or super-women (or asexual or bi-sexual beings) called "gods".

And again emerging from this concept or independently of it, there arose the idea of one almighty power—the "one god", omnipotent, omniscient, the mysterious and unseen creator of the universe.

*

If I believe in this one almighty power that created the world—and me—then surely I am not unreasonable in assuming that it was done for a purpose? If it does not have a reason, why is it?

And if I am here for a purpose, surely it is not unreasonable for me to assume that unless I know that purpose I cannot be blamed if I fail to fulfil it?

And if this power decrees laws which I must obey, how do I find out what they are for me now—not as they were apparently told to others thousands of years ago?

It is very perplexing—for I am told I am "sinning" even as I fail to commit my belief in this unseen almighty power.

*

And whosoever speaketh a word against the Son of man, it shall be forgiven him: but whosoever speaketh against the Holy Ghost, it shall not be forgiven him, neither in this world, neither in the world to come.
(Matthew, 12:32)

Please let me know what that means! If I am committing unforgivable sin in my ignorance . . . how diabolically unfair!

Could it be that I can only *really sin* when I *know* what sin *really* is?

*

However, presumably, if I do not so far believe in this almighty power—called "God", "Holy Ghost", or whatever—then neither will I believe that I can sin against "him". And I certainly will not believe that I can be punished "after death" because, for me, there is no almighty power to administer the punishment.

Does that not, therefore, free me once and for all from all fear of divine retribution?

I am thus free to indulge in whatever I wish without fear of any consequences (unless I break a man-made law and, even then, only if I am found out).

It does sound very tempting.

*

54

And (the devil) *saith unto him, All these things will I give thee, if thou wilt fall down and worship me.*

(Matthew, 4:9)

*

I wonder if I would be totally satisfied if I resolved simply to do and take just what I wanted, regardless of "god" or anyone else?

Could such a "philosophy" be reconciled with my capacity to "love"?

What is this capacity to "go out of myself to someone or something"?

What would happen if I denied my ability to "love"?

Where does it come from?

Why do I have it?

*

There are times when I "feel" so strongly about another human being that I could say "I love them more than I love myself" (which may not be too difficult!). I would not have him or her suffer "for all the world". Indeed, if they suffer, it upsets me—I suffer with them. And if I were to make them suffer because of something I had said or done, then my suffering would be worse.

But, if I suffer, how do I suffer? Not through infliction from outside myself. I am not imprisoned or exiled or executed just for loving (though my actions motivated by that love may invite considerable hostility!). It is, as it were, a self-inflicted suffering. I suffer within. And this emotional, inner turmoil may be so intense that I will feel imprisoned in my mind, exiled from the loved one and "crucified" by my anguish or my regret or my guilt.

But, if my love is received and welcomed, is there any joy and happiness like it? Is there anything to equal the "surrendering" to it? In this state, I am liberated, utterly belong, "come to life". What would I not sacrifice for the loved one?

*

And I do not confine this desire to love just to sexual attraction. That may play a part in it—but it is not the whole story.

55

I find I experience deep love for other people—my parents or friends or those I respect and admire. I simply "love" them. I get on well with them. I respond or react in harmony with them. I enjoy their companionship. I can be in a state of communion with them. I "go out of myself" to them.

Why should this be? I do not usually ask myself. Nor does it necessarily last for long. But when I am in this state, I feel a "whole" lot better than when I am out of it.

Come to think of it, there are times when I feel this warmth for a person who does not even notice me, who may not know me at all.

And then there are times I feel "love" when no other person is involved at all.

Suddenly, for no apparent reason, I feel in harmony with anything and everything. I am "in love with life". I am in an all-embracing state of "well-being".

What on earth is going on? How can it be? Why is it not like it all the time?

In that moment of "being in love"—whether it is because of a person or for no apparent reason—I do not want anything; I do not find myself wanting anything. (How much this is in contrast to the idea that, if I want to, I can do and take whatever I wish.)

It is as though in some mysterious way, by some strange alchemy apparently out of my control, I am suddenly made complete.

It is as if I am made *whole*.

*

They that are whole have no need of a physician . . .

*

Now, is it that, at that moment, I have been given something— some attitude, some idea, some understanding—that I did not have before? Did this love come to me from somewhere else?

Or, is it that all the rest of the time—when I am "out of love", when I am preoccupied mentally and physically with my day to day concerns, when I am involved with myself—it is simply that I have forgotten ("got" something "for" or "instead of")? Am I in some way "sick" when it is not there?

In other words, am I *given* love from time to time? Or is it always there but I am usually not able to *give myself to* it?

One thing is certain—no one can tell me to "fall in love"; no one else can tell me to experience love; I cannot even command myself to love. It seems that sometimes I just happen to feel *wholly* in love.

And all the time that I do not feel "whole", part of me is never at rest; part of me is always desiring for all kinds of things which are supposedly lacking; part of me, like "a longing in the heart", pines to retrieve the elusive "wholeness".

Does it mean that something I am doing, thinking, believing, is cutting me off from it?

Why am I "without" it?

*

What is the difference between "being in love with someone" and "loving someone"?

*

If I am whole, then clearly there is nothing extra that I want, there is nothing further that I need.

I do not need to prove anything, or achieve anything, or even do anything—in my own interest.

I am completely and utterly content in the present moment.

Then something happens to interfere—and my mind chases off coping with the interference and trying to restore the equanimity. The sense of well-being is lost and I become fragmented—involved in a multitude of demanding and varied things. Desires for what I think I want take me away, as it were, from the sense of completeness. I assume that if I satisfy my desires, the sense of wholeness will return. But does it?

I fail to notice that the essential quality of the wholeness has got nothing to do with desires satisfied. In it, there is no "me" motivating anything.

Where is the desiring "me" when "I" am whole?

*

57

This surely cannot mean that there should be no desire?

But perhaps the degree and quality of my desiring will change when I cease to be fooled by my belief that their gratification will provide any lasting satisfaction?

*

There is an old moral brain-teaser which goes something like this:

If you could have your greatest desire, if you could have your most heart-felt wish come true, and all you had to do was simply press a button and somewhere in the world a man, whom you had never met nor knew anything about, would die as a direct result of your action . . . would you do it?

The answer must surely depend upon the strength of your desire, upon the importance to you of having your wish come true? And it must also depend, on the other hand, on the strength of your sense of moral law, on how you value "life"?

What, for example, if someone you loved dearly would only continue to live if you took the life of someone else?

*

When Jesus speaks about sin, is he talking about offending man-made law?

Or is he suggesting that to sin is simply to remain in a state that is not truly and completely "whole", through failing to understand?

If the latter is the case, then that must surely mean that I can only sin against *myself* (or rather, the "Holy Ghost" within myself)? In which case, my suffering is of course inevitable, unforgivable— because I automatically bring the "punishment" *on myself* by the folly of my actions.

*

If I, as an individual, am not quite the same as any other living being, then, when I am "whole", will I be any less individual? Am I less whole *to myself* if I am white instead of black, short rather than tall, thin rather than fat? Am I any less whole *to myself* if I cannot speak a foreign language, if I am no good at mathematics,

58

if I cannot sing in tune? Am I any less whole if I do not know what someone else means by faith or if I do not believe in another man's concept of the god-idea? Will not my "wholeness" be individual? I could add tomorrow all kinds of possessions and achievements to what I have and am today—but would they make me any more "whole" *to myself* than I am *now*?

Is it possible that "wholeness" is to do with my *being* completely myself, here and now?

If I am not fragmented and scattered in my mind, I am whole.

"I am I".

*

The codes of conduct, which it is a "sin" to contravene, may be useful guide-lines for the aspiring Christian—and strictly obeying them may make him feel righteous (or pleased and self-satisfied)—but if I obey the rules without understanding them and they do not make me feel "whole" (truly "holy"), if I obey them and yet still feel vulnerable, disturbed, deprived, anxious, fearful, unenlightened, unfulfilled . . . what value is there in that?

Can anyone else make me "whole"—or rather, can anyone else stop me from desiring the things that prevent me from realizing that I am already "whole"?

Can you see through my eyes?

Can you hear through my ears?

Can you touch, taste, smell through my body?

Does anyone know anything exactly as I know it?

Can you commit my sins?

Can you do my dying for me?

Can you *be* me?

Who then can make me whole?

*

Likewise, no one can repent for me. Only I can repent for my sins—when I have understood the nature and manner of my sinning.

*

What is conscience?
Do I have one?
Does everyone have one?
Have I "heard" my conscience?

Conscience seems to me to be that influencing, inner sense that "tells" me what is right or wrong. I realize that sometimes it is very difficult to know whether I am "hearing" my conscience or simply responding with a conditioned, indoctrinated, acquired learning of what is right and wrong. Perhaps it is that if the two criteria coincide, then I will not be able to distinguish one from the other. But, if they are in conflict, then I will know the difference. I may have been conditioned to believe that it is right to kill an enemy in self-defence or in the defence of my community; but when my finger is cold-bloodedly on the trigger . . .

It is not at all easy to know exactly what governs my behaviour in different circumstances. For sure, the only hope of finding out is to observe my experience through life and to learn the lessons it teaches.

But, maybe I have known that experience of "hearing a voice within"? Sometimes I have known undeniably what I should or should not do in a certain situation, often long before I have tried to work out whether the decision is sensible or not.

Conscience means "with knowledge". What is this knowledge, this inner conviction? What is this intuitive "voice" which "tells" me?

*

If I feel that I have fallen in any way short of what is natural, loving and in harmony, then I had better examine what has happened. If I regret some foolishness or mistake, maybe I allow the possibility of repentence?

I may not concern myself with what others say about how I should behave and conduct myself, but what do *I* expect of *my self*? Do I have any standards to set *my self*? Or do I continually justify myself and explain away my shortcomings?

Where do these expectations I have of *my self* come from? Is it conscience again, calling me to give account of *my self*?

*

In Thomas' Gospel, there is a "saying of Jesus":

Jesus said: Why do you wash the outside of the cup? Do you not understand that he who made the inside is also he who made the outside?

(Thomas, Log. 89)

*

When I try to discover the essence of the Christian concept of sin, am I dealing with the *outside* of the cup—how it looks—or the *inside*—how it meets what is required of it?

Am I primarily concerned with how I conduct myself outside, in the world's eyes; or inside, where none except I can see?

Or, if *I am* the cup . . .

What use is the outside without the inside, or the inside without the outside?

*

To sin or not to sin may be the crucial factor in my search for my true self; sinning may be the obstacle that stands between *me*, the incomplete, and the real *I*, the whole one . . .

And, if it is so crucial, I need to understand very precisely what is meant by it.

To sin must be realized as an intensely personal experience— not just a question of the world's judgement on me. What is sin for me may not be sin for you; I cannot judge you and you cannot judge me. And what is sin at one moment may give rise to a leap into "wholeness" at another, if I realize the sinning.

*

But go ye and learn what that meaneth, I will have mercy, and not sacrifice: for I am not come to call the righteous, but sinners to repentance.

(Matthew, 9:13)

61

Five

Then was Jesus led up of the Spirit into the wilderness to be tempted of the devil.

And when he had fasted forty days and forty nights, he was afterwards an hungred.

And when the tempter came to him, he said, If thou be the Son of God, command that these stones be made bread.

But he answered and said, It is written, Man shall not live by bread alone, but by every word that proceedeth out of the mouth of God.

Then the devil taketh him up into the holy city, and setteth him on a pinnacle of the temple,

And saith unto him, If thou be the Son of God, cast thyself down: for it is written, He shall give his angels charge concerning thee: and in their hands they shall bear thee up, lest at any time thou dash thy foot against a stone.

Jesus said unto him, It is written again, Thou shalt not tempt the Lord thy God.

Again, the devil taketh him up into an exceeding high mountain, and sheweth him all the kingdoms of the world, and the glory of them;

And saith unto him, All these things will I give thee, if thou wilt fall down and worship me.

Then saith Jesus unto him, Get thee hence, Satan: for it is written, Thou shalt worship the Lord thy God, and him only shalt thou serve.

Then the devil leaveth him, and, behold, angels came and ministered unto him.

(Matthew, 4:1-11)

How, I wonder, did I first learn the rules and laws of my community?

Initially, I suppose, they came to me from my parents or guardians. At the same time that I was learning certain things through my senses—for instance, that fire could burn me—they were teaching me mainly by example, perhaps unaware that they were doing so, the language and custom of their society. Not only did I learn the general rules applicable to the whole society but also the particular rules of behaviour belonging to my section of it. In other words, I was conditioned generally by the society into which I was born; and I was conditioned more specifically according to the role and status of my parents in that society.

This process—subtly inculcated and unquestioned at the time—gave me the standards, values and therefore the basis of judgement, with which to cope with my experience.

*

My first beliefs as to what was right and wrong, good and bad, truth and untruth—and all the other dual aspects that presented themselves for evaluation and judgement in my mind—were introduced to me by my parents. Naturally it was assumed that I would adopt these standards and values—simply because my parents held them and they were therefore presumably the best criteria.

Later, when I went to school, my teachers continued this process of indoctrination. I may have been perplexed by the occasional belief that seemed alien to mine but, in the main, the codes of behaviour established in the home were endorsed in school.

Thus I received the early instruction as to what I should and should not do. It was probably a fairly painless education during those first years. I did not suffer unduly if I transgressed. I may have been rebuked and occasionally punished ("for my own good" they would say) but, on the whole, my misdemeanours were not taken all that seriously.

At this stage, I knew *when* I was disobeying the rules that I had been taught and had had to accept as inflexible; but I did not know *why* I had to obey many of them nor how relative or inadequate they might be. I simply did not have the mental capacity nor the experience to question or dispute them.

*

As I grew older things began to take a more serious turn. I had to become more accountable for my activities, to become more responsible.

Now I had more specific tasks to attend to and greater discipline to observe. There was more and more learning to be absorbed; more being tested in one form or another to see if I was making the necessary effort. I was introduced to all kinds of subjects—regardless of whether I was interested or not. They were, I was told, the necessary grounding required for me to be able to take my place in the world. Increasingly, breaking the rules was becoming less a case of damaging my own interests and more one of threatening the well-being of others.

I was also now, hopefully, beginning to employ and develop my particular talents. I was beginning to realize my own abilities, discover my own special interests, establish my own recognizable identity. I was beginning to express my individuality and to explore and expand my "territory".

I also began to question some of the rules; and became conscious of the fact that they were in general necessary—but not indisputable.

As a child, I had tended to accept everything as it happened; you could say that it had been a simple and straightforward life in that it had been totally directed by others. But now I was experiencing dualism; the emerging "individual" was being confronted with increasingly serious choices and decisions.

*

However, whatever branch of learning I was following (with a view to "earning a living", both for the benefit of myself and the community) and in whatever ways I was become distinct among my contemporaries because of my successes and failures, in one respect we all remained the same. We were all, in general, subject to the same law. Everything any of us could do had to be within a certain boundary of permission.

And that was not just the statutory laws of the society. No matter how differently we were forming as individuals, we all had the same responsibility to cope with the same principles of right and wrong, good and bad, truth and untruth. We were all subject to the same threat of judgement and punishment.

Whatever any of us said and did, we now had responsibility. But responsibility to what? To the state or community to which we belonged. But just that? Surely there was more to the "ability to respond" than that?

Upon what depends the dignity and worth of a man?

*

During the formative period of my life—first with my parents and then with my teachers—I may also have been introduced to the moral and ethical beliefs of the religions upheld by my society.

My parents may have had no interest in religion as such, and neither may my teachers, but so bound together are the laws of the community and the laws of religious tradition that none of us can avoid exposure to the latter when learning the former (unless it happens to be a state founded on an atheistic ideology).

Thus to break the laws of society is both a "crime" socially and very often a "sin" religiously.

So, even if I have received little or no religious instruction, I am none the less influenced by persuasions that have moral or religious foundation. And I would be aware of the concept of responsibilities beyond those of my immediate environment—to people unknown to me, to society in general, to humanity as a whole; and possibly to the "god" of my religion.

*

If a society dispenses with the god-idea, it inevitably invests all power in itself, i.e. in its members, i.e. in man himself.

Can man have become so self-assured and incorruptible that he can now presume to do such a thing?

Certainly man may have reached a stage of maturity where he can dispense with superstitious fear and scape-goat "gods"; but can he ever afford to ignore and deny the cause of himself?

*

So, I reach an age, say somewhere between eleven and fourteen—when I begin to specialize in my interests and become increasingly individual. And I begin to have to make decisions for myself. And I begin to realize "I am".

Here I stand—with a background conditioning of the law, the tradition, the history, the mythology and the ideology of my parents, my family, my teachers, my community and its religious establishment, all stored away in my memory, picked up arbitrarily and inconsistently over the years. According to my interpretations of their meaning, they are reflected in my attitudes, my beliefs and my behaviour.

However dependable and comprehensive the collection I have made, I am now faced with having to play an active part in the world. It is expected of me that I should know what I ought and ought not to do, what I should and should not want, what I propose to be and do in life.

The difficulty is that I do not know in advance how well equipped I am to take on this responsibility.

*

And, at around this same stage in my life—simultaneously and significantly—something else is happening.

Called the age of puberty, I reach what the dictionary would tell me is "the beginning of sexual maturity".

Physically, I have reached the time when I can play an active role in the reproduction of the species, in the creating of human life.

What a thought! But no matter how seriously I think about it,

66

can I really grasp the import of it? That there should be emerging in me the possibility of being a parent myself, of another being.

*

The emergence in the young body of sexual potency has, of course, many varied and far-reaching effects in body and mind.

I can only observe as, entirely beyond my control, the body changes—as do those of my contemporaries.

As boys experience the approach of manhood, their voices deepen, facial and body hair grows, the body itself changes shape . . .

And as girls approach womanhood, the breasts form, the monthly cycle in the womb starts, the body also changes shape . . .

I become acutely aware of these changes. The effect of this "chemical" explosion in my system has widespread repercussions on what I think and how I think. I seem to shift to a new viewpoint on life and I become more critical, of myself and others, and more conscious, of myself and others. The self-criticism manifests in concern as to how I look, how impressive I am, how successful I am; in my increasing self-consciousness, I start to be concerned about my image—how to avoid appearing naive, foolish, ignorant.

I am moving out of my child role—and know little of the adult role I am moving into.

*

As I become more self-critical and self-conscious, so my individuality asserts itself, with both its strengths and its weaknesses. My attitudes change and my opinions become more forceful.

I no longer rely to the same extent on my parents and guardians. I may continue to love them, and I may be aware that they love me . . . but they can also irritate and anger me. They seem to think that I am still a child! Do they not realize how much I am changing?

And the rules to which I am subject cease to be taken so much for granted. I criticize them for being restrictive—and some of them seem absurd, even perverse. The rules may be all right for *them*; *they* made them as far as I am concerned. But why should I have to accept them? The older generations do not seem to allow that

67

I have the outlook of my generation; adults are old people with out-dated ideas about life.

I begin to realize that any authority is not absolute and may be suspect; if I want to, I can challenge it; and, if I feel strongly enough, I can rebel against it.

*

And so I fall in with those friends of my own age who share my interests, who think the way I do, those who will recognize my problems, whose outlook harmonizes with mine.

From among these friends, there emerge one or two, the best friends, and with them I form deep and committed relationships. It is through them that I learn to appreciate the reward of sharing and giving.

At first, the friendships tend to be with my own sex, for the opposite sex seems to have different rules and interests. With my close friends I can share the repercussions of the physical maturing, the changing emotions, the changing ideas about life, the romantic hopes and the personal fears, the love and the hate, the excitement and the disappointment—and the deep questions which I may now begin to experience.

There is so much to discuss. The whole world is waiting to be discovered and conquered from my new-found, maturing viewpoint. The whole enigma of life waits to be unravelled . . .

I become aware of the variety of people and their particular habits and attitudes. Some seem to be passive and introspective—accepting the system and totally subject to it; others seem to be active and extrovert—resenting all authority and being openly rebellious. Some seem to take life so seriously; others do not seem to be at all impressed and treat life as a joke.

And me? What am I doing? What is my choice? Where do I stand in this diversity?

I am *questioning* . . .

*

It is not that I have not questioned before; no, not at all. As a child I never stopped questioning:

68

How do flowers grow? How does a bird fly? What is light? How do the stars shine? What happens to dead people? Where do babies come from? . . .

And the world gave me its answers; and I believed.

But now, as I become increasingly aware of myself, the questions are dominantly about myself; they change as I change.

What is happening to me? Why do I feel like this? What am I here for? How do I find happiness? What happens if I die? Why am I the way that I am?

*

It is a period of great possibilities—and turmoil.

"Why?" I ask, about so many things . . .

Part of me is still a child, glad to retreat into the comfort and security of the familiar, willing to obey the rules, realizing that I must yet depend on the protection and support of my parents and teachers.

Part of me is striving to be independent, frustrated by the restrictions on freedom, wanting to go my own way, do what I please, rely on my own judgement.

Who are these "two"—the one who wants to stay at home and the one who wants to go out into the world?

Increasingly I feel the pulls of this way and that, suffering all manner of dilemma and duality—can, cannot; should, should not; want, do not want; hope, fear; like, dislike; love, hate.

How difficult it is to be sure, to be consistent, to be simply happy!

No wonder I question what is going on. No wonder I try to find out if anyone knows the answers to the perplexities.

*

Then was Jesus led up of the Spirit into the wilderness to be tempted of the devil.

*

It is during this period, when there often does not seem anything stable or constant to trust and nowhere to turn, that religion can assume a new significance.

Because I am sometimes bewildered and confused by the questions and the choices, and because I need to find something to rely on, the god-idea and the religious life can attract my attention.

I am presented with the idea "god"—a divine being, an almighty power, the cause of everything, call "him" what you will—who will understand my predicament and to whom I can turn wholeheartedly for help. If I try hard enough to obey his instruction, surrender my will to him, worship him . . . all my questions will be answered, my doubts and fears removed, my confusion and unrest dissolved. I can speak to him privately (through prayer), explain my troubles, confide my fears and put my trust where it cannot be betrayed. And I can look for all the support I need from his official representatives here on earth.

If I have been brought up in a mainly Christian community and family, then most probably I will pray to the Christian "God" and will seek for guidance through the Christian tradition—either through priests of the Church or through devout believers.

But I will not obtain this salvation for nothing. There will be no divine help if I am an unrepentant sinner. I have to learn how to conduct myself as a Christian if I am to receive forgiveness and absolution.

*

I discover that traditional religion has much to say about what I am experiencing during puberty and that the sin concept is closely linked with sexual maturity and all its ramifications—with all the attendant desires and temptations, the urge to love and be loved, the pursuit of satisfactions both obviously and subtly linked with sexual fulfilment.

I learn that procreation through union of the male and female is a "gift of God" and that it must not be abused through selfish gratification; it is a sacred union, not only because of the relationship of the two people involved, but because another "life" may be involved also.

I am told that many times and in many ways I will be tempted to "sin against God" and that I must resist these temptations.

I am told to honour my parents; yet what if I have to deceive them or hurt them in order to be of help to a friend who is dear to me? Or if I have to inconvenience or disobey them in order to attend the church?

What if I have to tell a lie in order not to offend or disappoint a friend?

What if I cannot help disliking someone who has undoubtedly offended me?

What if I want to acquire power and wealth in order that I may then help the poor and oppressed?

It is even a sin, I discover, to think evil thoughts. But how can I help it if they "come into" my head? How can I stop them?

*

There is a possibility that I shall "fall in love" with the Christ; that I shall find that I am able to have faith and to trust; that I shall be able to surrender my selfish will; that I shall love the services, the ceremonies and the rituals; that I shall happily confirm that I am a believer; that I shall feel duly honoured to be initiated into the rites that will enable me to commune with the almighty power.

On the other hand, the religious practice and its obligations and demands may only confuse me further. What can that jumble of incomprehensibilities mean? What relevance do they have to my life? On top of all my worldly concerns, how can I cope with the worry that I may be "sinning against God" or the fear that I am being "tempted by the devil"?

Far from religion undoubtedly being a help, it seems that it can also make matters worse!

*

Gradually, with increasing insistence, sexual desire asserts itself in my life. And, perhaps above all others at this time, I become aware of the strictures that society (and religion) would impose on its expression.

There is so much discussion and talk about sex around me; so much emphasis and importance is placed on it (and all the rituals and

71

practices associated with it—all those activities and acquisitions which enhance the chances of attraction and achievement). I cannot escape it unless I choose to become some sort of recluse, unless I opt for some form of life which deliberately excludes it. I inevitably become more and more curious; and the temptation increases to translate what I see and hear into practice.

How do I meet this "temptation"?

It will depend on how I have been conditioned in my childhood and education.

But, be "tempted" I undoubtedly will; and if I have any concept of its possibly being "sinful" then I will have anxiety.

Can I resist or not? Will I be sinning or not? What will my punishment be? What kind of law is it that seeks to repress a natural urge within me, an urge crying out for expression?

What is the point of a dilemma like that?

Is it some kind of trial instituted by "God" to teach me something? Or is it some legacy of man's erroneous thinking?

*

For sure, the Christ story *itself* provides no guidance.

How did Jesus cope with his own adolescence? What was he doing between the ages of twelve and thirty? Did he, by virtue of his incarnation, experience no such predicament? Did he have any idea what the experience is like for an ordinary mortal?

We do not know. For some strange reason, the chroniclers of his life tell us nothing of his adolescence.

Might that not be very significant?

*

If I have been much conditioned with beliefs about right and wrong, I will find my emergence into adolescence a very trying time. All the thinking and worrying about good and bad, all the decisions I am called upon to make, all the resisting "temptation"—it all becomes rather serious, and possibly wearying. And from what I see of the adult world, it does not appear that it is going to become easier later.

72

It seems only yesterday that life was a carefree game.

Now everything is "important" and I am being told that I am responsible for my future; it is "up to me". Even the fate of my "soul"—my spiritual "alter-ego", as it were—is at stake. I may go to "heaven"; I may invite "eternal damnation" and be cast into the "fires of hell".

I really do not know what any of it means.

*

But one thing may be clear to me in this situation—I am far from being "whole".

I am being pushed hither and thither in response to all kinds of influence and sometimes it seems that I play the roles of countless different "me"s, all wanting different things, frequently at logger-heads with each other . . . and all chasing each other around in my head.

What can I do about it?

Even my closest friends cannot resolve the confusion for me. The most they can do is sympathize—and they are not always ready to do that, for they have their own confusion to cope with.

There are times when I feel utterly alone.

No one can help me.

I am told that I can only help myself.

But, not knowing how to do that, I can only escape the predica-ment by throwing myself into the routines, demands and entertain-ments of each day. I must enjoy what I can.

Maybe I will find the answer . . . tomorrow.

Perhaps it depends on how "hungry" I become.

*

And when he had fasted forty days and forty nights, he was afterwards an hungred.

*

There are times when the future seems to be all mapped out for me.

73

I will do well at school; I will leave and find a good job—something suited to my talents or aptitudes; I will get married—to someone suited to my temperament and personality; I will become a parent to children; I will look after them until they are old enough to lead their own lives; I will grow old, as comfortably as possible; I will then die.

All that I have to contribute to this ordered plan is obedience to the laws of the state, responsibility to my partner in marriage, hard work in my job, loving care for my children and resigned acceptance of my fate and limited life-span.

Nor need all this be dull; not at all. If things go "right", I can congratulate myself and enjoy the success of my achievements; I can enjoy the love and companionship of my partner, my children and my friends; there are many pleasures and entertainments to be found; and then, health and doctor permitting, I can "slip quietly away".

And, if things go "wrong", life will not be dull either! It may just be that I shall be less reluctant to leave.

*

It may be the most sensible course—and probably less wearing—not to enquire too much and just get on with life as best I can.

But how will I cope if the plan does go badly awry?

And what, in any case, if for *me* the plan will not suffice?

Did I really come into this world with no greater potential than just to conform to a predictable pattern?

If I did, then why do I have questions to disturb me, dreams to entice me, fears to haunt me and yearning to discomfort me?

*

Is the predictable pattern, the inexorable passage from the cradle to the grave, all that "life" has to offer?

There is presumably nothing "wrong" with leading such a life; but how do I evaluate it?

I may become rich, successful, famous, exceptionally learned—but will it guarantee happiness? What is the point if it all vanishes into thin air when I die? It might benefit others? Does that just mean that, at best, my deeds will make it a little easier for others to complete the course of their lives?

If I concentrate on getting the most that I can out of life, I may, in passing, learn many things about life and myself? But what is that experience really teaching me? Can it be any use to me when I am dead? And if it is of potential use to me when I am alive, what is the nature of that use? If I do not realize anything from the experience —some revelation about the purpose of my life—does it matter whether I am a success or a failure, a "good" person or a "bad" person?

*

But (Jesus) *answered and said, It is written, Man shall not live by bread alone, but by every word that proceedeth out of the mouth of God.*

*

However the questions as to the purpose of life are answered, we may come closer to understanding the fundamental choice from the story of the "temptation in the wilderness".

As we experience and consider the dilemmas in life, we may see that at root they are all to do with having to choose between either serving "my" interests or serving an interest "outside myself". For the sake of descriptive labels, we might term the voice that calls us to serve selfless purposes "god-like" while the voice that tempts me to give precedence to my interests "devilish". It appears that the former usually calls for effort (primarily to resist the temptation of the other voice) whilst the latter appeals to courses of action which are self-indulgent and more immediately rewarding.

Sometimes it may not be so simple to distinguish which is which; the mind is very good at explanations, justifications and thoroughly confusing the issue. And may not such machinations of the mind be indicative of the cunning of the "devil"? "Altruistic" actions can so easily be motivated by self-interest; and apparently "selfish" actions can sometimes be altruistic.

These are processes that I have to observe *in myself* and resolve *for myself.* No one else can enter my mind and decide what is going on there! Likewise, it is not my business to judge anyone else.

And then, when I have watched and listened—especially to the consequences of my words and actions—maybe I will understand what it is that I can genuinely serve and "worship".

*

Then saith Jesus unto him, Get thee hence, Satan: for it is written, Thou shalt worship the Lord thy God, and him only shalt thou serve.

*

During puberty, I am beset by all manner of doubts, fears and questions. I begin to become aware of myself and aware of the duality within my mind. I need to love and I need to be loved.

It is as though I am an open book, waiting to be written upon. When I was a child, other people wrote the "introduction"; now the writing of the real book is being done by me.

If there is sin in *me*, then it is *my* sin, and I must recognize it and deal with it. That is *my* responsibility; *I* am responsible for *my self.*

*

And, perhaps, according to my response-ability, I shall discover the secret of "being in love".

*

Jesus said: If you bring forth that within yourselves, that which you have will save you.

If you do not have that within yourselves, that which you do not have within you will kill you.

(Thomas, Log. 70)

76

Six

And seeing the multitudes, he went up into a mountain: and when he was set, his disciples came unto him:
And he opened his mouth, and taught them, saying,
Blessed are the poor in spirit: for theirs is the kingdom of heaven.
Blessed are they that mourn: for they shall be comforted.
Blessed are the meek: for they shall inherit the earth.
Blessed are they which do hunger and thirst after righteousness: for they shall be filled.
Blessed are the merciful: for they shall obtain mercy.
Blessed are the pure in heart: for they shall see God.
Blessed are the peacemakers: for they shall be called the children of God.
Blessed are they which are persecuted for righteousness' sake: for theirs is the kingdom of heaven.
Blessed are ye, when men shall revile you, and persecute you, and shall say all manner of evil against you falsely, for my sake.
Rejoice, and be exceeding glad: for great is your reward in heaven: for so persecuted they the prophets which were before you.

(Matthew, 5:1-12)

*

As my formal education draws to an end, I become more and more involved in my social environment.

I have reached the stage when my survival no longer entirely depends on being cared for by my parents nor upon the guidance of my teachers: I am beginning to "look after" myself.

The community to which I belong now begins to make demands;

77

I am expected to play a part, in no matter how lowly a role, in its welfare. I must now become a responsible member of the tribe.

During the latter days of my education, my endeavours have been aimed mainly at acquiring sufficient learning or skill to equip me for a "job" through which I shall be able to "earn a living". I am about to start working—and the only work that will support me has to be something that the community *requires*.

If I cannot find such work, then, perhaps, the community will support me—but only as long as there is literally no work. I will be under constant pressure to do something, anything, that will contribute to the welfare—the wealth, health and survival—of the community.

*

What a shift this seems from my childhood world. Maybe in many ways I wanted to grow up, to be able to do the things adults do, but I did not really appreciate the implications of having to "earn a living". Indeed, the emphasis had been far more towards having been "given my life".

Now, it seems, the gift was really a loan—and that now I have to pay back to society for the support it gave me during my infancy and for the privilege of now belonging to it.

And yet, my very existence here, my very presence in the world, appears to have come about through the random desire of my parents.

Did I choose to be here? Did I have any say in the matter?

I wonder?

If not, then why should I be expected to "earn a living"?

If I did not ask to come, it hardly seems fair to have to work now that I am here.

*

So, I must earn a living.

However, there is, as always, a dual aspect to this situation. For, in whatever capacity I am working for the needs of the community, I am also working for myself.

78

I have already noticed during my school days that I am often loath to meet my responsibilities and that I am a creature of wishes and desires. I have already seen that sometimes I am lazy and cannot be bothered, especially if I am being asked to make an effort to do something I do not want to do. "I do not care," I say. And I have seen that sometimes I am capable of considerable effort, especially if it is directed towards the things, the many things, that I want to possess or do.

Most of the "things" that I desire will not just come to me if I sit around waiting for them; I have to go out and get them.

*

I may, if I am lucky, actually satisfy my desires through doing the work I do.

For, as I have noticed, I may have a "vocation"—some activity that will afford me a living and which at the same time suits me as well.

I may want to be a doctor or a nurse, and thus help the sick and the suffering—through an understanding of the laws that govern the body and the mind.

I may want to be a lawyer, or an administrator, or a politician, and thus contribute to the order and running of the community—through an understanding of the laws that regulate human conduct and economics.

I may want to be a representative of the Church—interpreting the divine laws and serving the spiritual needs of the community.

I may want to be a scientist—fascinated by the natural laws that govern phenomena, laws of energy exchange and of cause and effect, and thus make contribution to mankind's "progress".

Or I may want to employ my aptitude for certain skills. I may become a farmer or a gardener, providing food for the community by harnessing the laws of nature, of the soil and the seasons.

I may want to design and construct buildings to house the multifarious needs of the community, through exploring the laws of materials and structure.

I may enjoy making things—clothes, furniture, pots, pans . . .

Or I may simply want to be married, to look after a home, to look after children, to teach children . . .

There are so many "vocations".

So long as there is a demand in the society and I can supply the demand, then the society will pay me for my service. I will be satisfactorily "earning my living".

What is vital about such "vocations" is that—to a greater or lesser degree—if I am engaged in one of them, then I am doing what I *want* to do. I am pursuing my "calling" and I am being paid for the pursuit.

*

But, on the other hand, what if people have no such vocation?

What if there is no job supplying the needs of the community that they *want* to do?

Perhaps they have a talent or a skill but it is latent or not sufficiently developed for them to be able to earn a living by it. It may simply remain as a hobby, something with which to amuse themselves in their spare time.

But work for their living they surely must—it is a cardinal rule of the tribe. If it is not obeyed then, in order to survive, such people may have to depend on charity, on begging; or they may resort to stealing—taking what they have not earned. This the community will not tolerate and they have to live with the fact that they are effectively outcast, criminal, parasitic . . . and so on.

So, whereas people with a vocation appear to be doing what they want to do, others may have to commit themselves to toil in some tedious and distasteful job, simply to keep their place in society and be accepted by it.

How unfair this seems. Why are people set apart in this way? Why cannot everyone simply do what they want to do?

*

Today, most societies in the world have become so complex that, in order to survive, a whole host of necessary tasks have to be attended to (some of which are a product of modern living, some of which in earlier times people used to perform for themselves).

Machines have to be put together and kept running. Coal and oil have to be extracted from under the earth or sea. Refuse has to be collected and disposed of. Food has to be mass-produced and packaged. Shops have to be supplied and staffed. Accounts have to be kept and taxes collected. Money has to change hands. People have to be supervised, policed and sometimes imprisoned. Men and arms have to be prepared to defend the community.

A lot of unattractive work has to be done by someone. Instead of everyone doing what they want to do, many have to be society's "slaves".

*

For every one who has the fortune to be following a vocation of his choice, there are countless numbers performing menial, boring, unfulfilling, repetitive jobs—simply to survive in the society to which they belong.

And then, there is no guarantee that a vocation will provide the continuing satisfaction that was first imagined. What happens for example if a person does not succeed in the vocation, finds that its promises are not fulfilled in practice, decides that after all it was the wrong vocation, is constantly frustrated by all manner of interference and pressure? And even if "successful", how sound or hollow is the success?

Has something gone wrong? If there is such widespread discontent, is there some factor in modern times which is being over-looked? Why is there such turmoil and violence in the world? Why are people finding it so difficult to live in harmony?

So acute is this situation becoming that it seems at times that we are all sitting on a huge volcano, waiting for the eruptions and rumblings that we hear in all directions to break out into one terrible holocaust.

Why?

How has it come about that a vast proportion of humanity is

committed, for a sizeable part of their waking lives, to engage in activities which are unpleasant, unfruitful and unbecoming to the dignity of man?

Has man done something—or failed to do something—that he should have deserved this situation?

Might it have something to do with the almost universal notion that if man can produce more and more wealth, then eventually everyone will have enough to satisfy him? Is this a vicious circle, a suicidal illusion?

Do we hear an echo of the "temptation in the wilderness"— "And (the devil) saith unto him, All these things will I give thee, if thou wilt fall down and worship me"?

*

Why should we, if we were born innocent, find ourselves in such a world of discontent?

Are we suffering the consequences of past folly?

If so, what can we do about it?

We can *question.*

And cease to subscribe to what we discover to be the untruth.

*

The whys and wherefores, the history and the explanations, need not concern us here—simply because they have nothing to do with *our* quest *now.* We cannot change the past; but we may rectify our present outlook.

*

If, for a moment, I can drop all my ideas, my preconceptions, my assumptions, my opinions, my habitual beliefs, about the world, about people, about the social and economic structures around me, then . . . are not all normal babies born equal—equal in potential, equally innocent, equally whole?

If it can be said that one baby is born with a vocation—then must not all babies have a potential vocation?

If one child has intelligence—then have not all children?

If one child can be called beautiful—then are not all children beautiful?

How do I come to think otherwise?

Who says what is intelligent, what is beautiful, what is useful?

*

Education has to be concerned with teaching facts, figures, laws, processes and skills; but it falls short of its prime responsibility if it does not encourage the pupil (or disciple, "one who learns") to discover his or her sense of value, sense of proportion and sense of humour (in its broadest sense of being able to maintain a balanced view, rectifying immoderate and extreme behaviour). In other words, education should encourage the individual to find for himself or herself his or her *own* possibilities and responsibilities in life. One could say that "education" which inculcates and indoctrinates ("in-ducts" rather than "e-ducts") is the complete reverse of what it should be.

For upon how I discover the ability to value, so will depend my valuation, my "view", of the world, the people in it, and what they say and do. And, above all, upon it will depend how I value myself and what I say and do.

Law and facts may control and inform my behaviour in life. But they cannot dictate to me how I value the worth of anything, how I value my experience, whatever experience happens to come my way. That ability I have to discover, explore and develop for myself. The danger of failing to do so is that I may be led indiscriminately into all manner of false belief.

From this point of view, how I happen to "earn a living" is, in itself, of little importance. What is crucial is whether I am able to evaluate what I am doing and how I am doing it.

Thus, we could say that the discontent among people, the discontent within myself, is due to the failure of being able to evaluate what is being thought, assumed, believed, said and done. Of course I shall be confused and disturbed if I am not able to distinguish truth from untruth, the worthy from the worthless, and so on. Of course I cannot help myself if I have not been taught how to help myself. It is no good telling me what is intelligent, beautiful or useful if I cannot realize it for myself. Otherwise, I am at the mercy of any persuasion, any nonsense.

*

It can be a complicated, confusing and challenging world that I find myself facing as I say good-bye to my childhood and set out on my career through life.

And there are times, although perhaps not often, when I wonder where "I" went to . . . for so quickly am I involved in the human "race" and I seem to have little time for what is deeply important to me.

It is a race—maybe a steeplechase—simply to keep going, and jumping, going and jumping—getting ahead, falling behind, catching up, keeping up . . . and going where? What is the hurry if the finishing post is death?

"We'll all be the same in a hundred years," they say, "we'll all be dead!"

What value then the money, the house, the car, the treasured possessions, the titles, the qualifications, the prizes . . . will it matter then that I never made a fortune, fulfilled the ambitions, won the accolades?

What use then the inspired idea that I had . . . or never had?

What then of the beauty of the world, or the ugliness, the happiness, or the unhappiness, the wishes come true, the desires denied?

Who can tell, in real and absolute terms, the value or worth of my life?

*

For, at the end, when death comes, what am I?

Am I more or less than I was at birth?

Am I the sum total of all my achievements and of all my short-comings? Am I just a memory, an epitaph, an obituary?

Am I my "virtues" and my "sins"?

Do I, when I am waiting for death, look back over my life—and echo the words of my youth: "What was it all for? Is that all there is to it?"

What a melancholy note to end on if that is so.

To have achieved so much in the eyes of the world—and then to be just a corpse.

Or to have achieved so little in the eyes of the world—so that it does not even notice when I have gone.

If we are all equal when we arrive at the mystery of birth into existence, and if we are all equal when we depart into the mystery of death . . . what is the point of the interim?

*

Take heed therefore how ye hear: for whosoever hath, to him shall be given; and whosoever hath not, from him shall be taken even that which he seemeth to have.

(Luke, 8:18)

*

But this simplistic view of life and death may be limited and dangerous thinking.

For, if I believe that all I have is an allotted life-span and that no matter what I do and achieve it will all be reduced to nothing by death, then I may take the view that I had better "get the most out of life". This may mean "enjoying" myself at every possible opportunity, doing what I want to do regardless of others, and at all costs trying to avoid pain and suffering.

There is an immediate problem here however; because if I decide to embark on this escapist, self-interested mode of living, then everyone else could start to do the same!

If I do something I want to do regardless of other people, then others may start doing things . . . regardless of me!

I may already have decided that it is not advisable for me to break the man-made laws of my community—for fear of the consequences; but there are many activities I discover—not in themselves unlawful—which may interfere with other people and be at their expense.

For example, I may be in a room that is hot and stuffy to me. Why should I not open the window?

But there is someone else in the room who likes hot and stuffy rooms and feels cold if the window is open.

If I open the window, why should they not immediately close it again?

The only obvious outcome of this minute social dilemma is that the two of us are in conflict and, though it may not come to the point of fighting to the death over it, then at least it will come to the point where one of us is going to suffer more than the other—and the "stronger" (the more determined in his own interest) will decide whether the window remains closed or is opened.

Certainly it is true to say that we will both be the same in a hundred years—neither relatively hot nor cold, but dead—but that, I fear, does not resolve the inconvenience for one of us in that room at that moment!

It is a minute example but, if I observe the world around me, I see the same conflict in operation in varying degrees of seriousness everywhere.

The conflict of opposing desires.

Both among people—and within myself.

*

Society, on its grander scale, often tries to combat the possibility of disintegration and chaos which would result from totally self-interested behaviour, by suggesting that we not only live and work for our community today but for the community of the future—for the generations yet unborn. We must work to improve the situation for our children, our children's children, and so on.

I must work today for a better tomorrow.

However altruistic this may seem (and however dubious I may be about it, in view of man's record of "improvement" over the centuries!), one thing is certain: if I am living and working for a

ot going to live that long, then I had
re is no real gain to be made through
my transitory benefit.

*

, religion may be seen to complement

asions, find it easy to work for this
be taking a long time to materialize!)
enefit when it is eventually achieved,
ragement and consolation.
ing in this life in order that I may
it, happiness and peace in the life

ill reap benefit in "heaven", where,
"recorded".

*

"hereafter"; work for others and for
two-pronged fork of "civilization",
the *modus operandi* and *vivendi* which will help me through from
the cradle to the grave.

And of course it makes some sense. It would not have become so
deeply rooted in the lore of the tribe—of all tribes—if it did not.
Without such inducement, the community would be hard put to
survive. The alternative to organization—anarchy—is a constant
threat.

But do I really understand it?

Is it a makeshift confidence trick?

Is there any other alternative?

*

It is possible that the conflict and friction of dualism gives rise
to, provides, the very energy necessary for development. It is the
very process which is the prerequisite of transformation.

Thus, is it possible that the dualistic concept of selfishness and
altruism is a dilemma within me that causes continual friction and

87

that this friction produces the necessary energy for the realization of its meaning? (If I were entirely passive and content, what stimulation or incentive would there be for potential development?)

Whether priest or layman, prime minister or dustman, worker or director, communist or capitalist . . . I am a human being—playing a part, and, like all actors, I may give a good or a bad performance.

What is important is that I *realize* I am playing a role—in the vast and complex phenomenon of human evolution in the biosphere. And it is not what I do but *how I do it*, the quality of the performance.

Then maybe I will understand . . . that the work itself is far "greater" than any explanation or motive that I may think I have for doing it.

*

Here I am; I do not in all honesty know where I came from; I do not know where I am going; I am here.

I do not even know why I am here.

But I do have one constantly available responsibility, a continuing point of reference, the instrument of life and work . . . *I* have *me*.

Regardless of my fate, my circumstances, socially or economically; regardless of my talents or my seeming lack of them; regardless of my intelligence, of my physical attributes, of my desires, my wishes, my achievements, my handicaps, my disappointments, my frustrations . . . *I* have *me*. *I* have to live with *me* all the time.

If *I* could begin to know *me*, really to *know*, then perhaps I would begin to understand my relationship with other people, my relationship with society, my relationship to work, my relationship to living, to religion, to the role I am performing.

If *I* could really understand *me*, I might not understand all lives, but I could begin to make sense of my life.

On the other hand, if I really did understand *my* life in its widest ramifications, I might understand *all life*, the *whole* of life.

*

What a challenge that is! . . . No longer doomed to the relentless pursuit of "other people's" desires, "other people's" ambitions, "other people's" achievements—for where did I acquire those ideas as to the desirability of riches, fame and accomplishment? Did I have them when I was born?

Withdrawn from relatively worthless pursuits, I am free to investigate, research and enquire into the most intriguing and amazing manifestation in the whole creation . . . me!

No one else can ever know me as I am capable of knowing me— once I take responsibility for myself.

By this, I do not mean morbid self-interest, self-concern, worrying about myself, withdrawn from the world; quite the opposite. I mean watching myself in relation to anything and everything. How else will I really know my responsibility?

And this knowing of yourself goes for everyone!

If I discover who I am, become conscious of the real *I* within me, the being at the very heart of myself, the one who can say "I am" and "I live" . . . then, when death comes, will I look back on a life of vain strivings, of fleeting moments of happiness, of "achievements" that never actually felt like achievements when they were reached? Or will I simply say "I am, and I know who I am", realizing that that is what really matters and that that was the purpose of my life? Especially if, during the process, I have become increasingly responsive to what I discover are the real needs around me during life.

"I am, and I know who I am. I am the life within me . . . "

Death may then indeed take life from *me*, just as birth gave life to *me*. But if I am the life itself . . .

It seems to *me* that life comes and life goes . . . but did *I* not come with it, and do *I* not depart with it? When life leaves, *I* leave.

It was *me* that was born and will die . . . *me*, the role-player, whose performance *I* watch.

*

It is all rather bewildering at first. I have always thought I am me.

My mind—or rather, what I call my mind—is so used to looking at the reflection in the mirror, *me*, that it has to be reminded, re-minded, that there is that, the real *I*, which is observing the reflection. (Do I not talk to myself, criticize myself, approve and disapprove of myself . . . Who is talking to, criticizing, approving, or disapproving of, myself?)

It is as if the "I" has to remember it is there, looking. (In just the same way that you may look at the reflection of yourself in the mirror and become so engrossed in it that you forget that you are there looking at it.)

Perhaps my mind can never *know* the answers to the profound questions in the way that it knows logical and scientific factual answers. The mind cannot know the cause of itself because it can only work with worldly terms—the terms that it has learned "in the world". It cannot reach out to a "time" before it was or a "place" where it has never been.

This rather suggests that the bewilderment and the confusion in the mind comes about through the intellect trying to work it all out, trying to do what it is not equipped to do. Maybe the intellect has limitations and there are ways of *knowing* things without there having to be worked out in the mind? Maybe the intellect has to learn that though it is very useful some of the time, there are times when it should keep still and stop filling the mind with thoughts— so that the mind, or rather, the reflecting instrument of mind, can simply reflect, contemplate, meditate upon.

"I" and "me" get very confused—*fused*—when the intellect tries to work out which is which. But let the mind reflect clearly—so that it sees that there is error in thinking the reflection to be the "reality". Reflections are but images, apparently *in* or *on* the surface of the mirror.

*

When my mind is "inspired" by an idea, it claims the inspiration —but, in all honesty, did my mind invent the inspiration or did it just receive it, as a gift?

Perhaps *I* am the inspiration of my mind.

Supposing my mind has been deceived by its worldly learning and

90

has mistaken an illusion for the reality? Supposing, in the same way that a mirror reverses the image of an object, my mind thinks in reverse.

Supposing *I* "chose" to be born.

And supposing my birth was a form of death, and that my death is a form of birth.

Does my future become my past, or does my past become my future?

*

Answerless questions. Or are they?

How can there be a question without an answer?

Which *did* come first—the chicken or the egg?

The logical, scientific intellect cannot "answer" that question.

Supposing the answer is the question . . . or rather, the answer is already there and is reflected as a question in the mind.

Supposing everything there ever will be, already is—waiting to be realized.

*

Blessed are the pure in heart, for they shall see God.

*

I am the specialist on *me*.

Only *I* am responsible for *me*.

Me questions; *I* answer.

In the illusion (in the "play" of life), *me* thinks all sorts of things about myself. But, in the same way that you are deceived if, when looking in the mirror, you say "That's me" and believe it, so *me* is deceived if it thinks it achieves, possesses, calls anything its own.

It is deceived if it thinks it can imagine and invent "god" and then choose to believe or not believe in the concept.

*

Blessed are the poor in spirit, for theirs is the kingdom of heaven.

*

Now a Christian "believer" may tell me that I am in danger of

91

"blaspheming" for I am apparently assuming the role of "god" for myself. That may be so—if I ascribe and claim for myself powers and privileges.

But am I doing this?

On the contrary, am I not beginning to realize that I have to divest myself of all pretence to any power or privilege in this world?

And he who tells me I blaspheme might perhaps be ascribing to himself powers of judgement which are not his to wield?

*

Blessed are they which do hunger and thirst after righteousness; for they shall be filled.

*

How do I hunger and thirst after righteousness?

Surely, by questioning, by searching for the truth.

One thing is becoming abundantly clear to me—my "righteousness" does not mean, nor depend upon, paying lip-service to another man's list of laws, list of beliefs, list of sins.

I do not want to be filled up with your idea of righteousness—any more than I want to persuade you to my idea of righteousness.

That will not make us *whole*. It will only add a bit more to the load of acquisitions that each of us is carrying round.

No; on the contrary; my "righteousness" surely depends on emptying myself of all acquired rubbish and listening intently again and again to my own doubts and uncertainties until I hear the basic *question* that underlies them.

And once I have heard that question, then only I can answer to it.

I must be patient and wait. This is when I need "faith"—to remain empty so that I can be filled.

*

Take ye heed, watch and pray: for ye know not when the time is.

For the Son of man is as a man taking a far journey, who left his house, and gave authority to his servants, and to every man his work, and commanded the porter to watch.

Watch ye therefore; for ye know not when the master of the house cometh, at even, or at midnight, or at the cockcrowing, or in the morning:
Lest coming suddenly he find you sleeping.
And what I say unto you I say unto all, Watch.

(Mark, 13:33-37)

*

Meanwhile, I may need to resist the temptation to settle for other men's ideas, opinions, beliefs, and convictions.

That does not mean rejecting them or ignoring them. Indeed, I need to be grateful for the offer of them and must consider them very carefully; they may well provide one of the "missing pieces" of my "jig-saw"; they may inspire my understanding.

But I must not take them and try to believe them.

*

I can study in a factory, in the market place, in a church, in the home, on top of a mountain—even if I were in prison.

I can study if I am happy and if I am miserable. I can study myself in comfort, in danger, in love, in fear, in confidence, in boredom, in anxiety, in excitement, in anguish . . .

Wherever I am, wherever I am going, whatever I am doing, I have myself with me. Always, I am watching, listening, waiting.

Always and in all places, I am my own persecutor. That does not mean I harass, criticize and punish myself—it means I "follow myself through" every moment that I remember.

Only then is there the possibility of purification, of throwing out the rubbish and the nonsense, of becoming clearly responsible to every need that I meet. Only then, may I be "made whole".

*

Blessed are they which are persecuted for righteousness' sake: for theirs is the kingdom of heaven.

Seven

And the third day there was a marriage in Cana of Galilee; and the mother of Jesus was there:

And both Jesus was called, and his disciples, to the marriage.

And when they wanted wine, the mother of Jesus saith unto him, They have no wine.

Jesus saith unto her, Woman, what have I to do with thee? mine hour is not yet come.

His mother saith unto the servants, Whatsoever he saith unto you, do it.

And there were set there six waterpots of stone, after the manner of the purifying of the Jews, containing two or three firkins apiece.

Jesus saith unto them, Fill the waterpots with water. And they filled them up to the brim.

And he saith unto them, Draw out now, and bear unto the governor of the feast. And they bare it.

When the ruler of the feast had tasted the water that was made wine, and knew not whence it was: (but the servants which drew the water knew;) the governor of the feast called the bridegroom.

And saith unto him, Every man at the beginning doth set forth good wine; and when men have well drunk, then that which is worse: but thou hast kept the good wine until now.

This beginning of miracles did Jesus in Cana of Galilee, and manifested forth his glory; and his disciples believed on him.

(John, 2:1–11)

*

The emergence of the sexual energy or force in me at puberty has profound effects on me, physically and mentally. I become more

94

conscious of myself. I "think things over to" myself and "keep things to" myself.

This is an internal debate and self-counselling that will stay with me, to a greater or lesser extent, for the rest of my life—particularly when pertaining to sexual matters, which gradually become the stimulating core from which springs so much of the motive for my actions. I am reluctant to share fully my observations and experiences with anyone, partly because I do not fully understand them myself and partly because I sense their potency and the need to be cautious and protective. They are part of my private world, a place where I can dream and weave my fantasies.

As I become increasingly aware of my physical attributes, at the same time I become more aware of other people's physique—particularly those older than myself, in the prime of their life. I am fascinated and identify with popular heroes in the worlds of entertainment, sport and adventure. Or I may idolize champions less remote—at school perhaps, or among my friends, or even just someone I see from time to time, in the neighbourhood.

This admiration and adulation can be for a member of either sex. He or she becomes my ideal. If the attraction is for a member of my own sex, then it is probably because I feel I would ideally like to develop their attributes, be as nearly like them as possible, emulate what they have succeeded in doing; in my eyes, they are the perfection of adulthood and represent what I can aspire to. If the attraction is for a member of the opposite sex, then that person represents the perfect "partner"; he or she is the embodiment of beauty and talent which I can worship. I feel I would do anything to win such a person—so that such a person could belong to me or I to them.

To such an extent am I charmed by such an idol or ideal that I want to be with that person, to share with that person, to devote myself to that person, to sacrifice myself to that person.

*

My heroes and heroines are of course all too often out of reach

95

and my dreams and fantasies about them are even more beyond the bounds of possible realization. But I need them; I have to have a vision or a goal to represent a direction and resolution for the powerful urges within me.

Reason may tell me that it is absurd to have such fantasies; and I may discover things about my "god" or "goddess" which tarnish their image and persuade me reluctantly to admit that such "perfection" is suspect and better worshipped from afar! But the heart is not easily deterred and I do so need those aspirations and dreams. My feelings have to be expressed somehow; the rising energy in my body cannot be suppressed.

What *is* going on?

Whatever it is, I cannot control nor deny its power and its invasion—its stimulation and its irresistible feelings and sensations. Periodically, it suddenly overwhelms me and it is as if I am "possessed" by it. It is far too intimate and possibly self-revealing for me to be able to discuss it with anyone. This is particularly so during the early stages of my new-found sexuality because the person who is the "object" of my feelings and dreams may be someone I know well and whom I fear would not respond sympathetically. Perhaps he or she would destroy my dream.

Even if I discover that other friends are going through much the same experiences, it does not really help or alter anything. It is impossible to talk openly and honestly about something so intensely personal and private.

*

Meanwhile, the pressure increases on all sides to meet my other responsibilities. I have to keep my sexual desires and my dreams of the ideal in check. I may be given to understand that I am as yet too young to be concerned with such things and that there are other more important responsibilities to apply myself to. And so my urges and dreams have to be put aside and they remain part of my secret life. I am alone with them; and, even if I wish I could, I cannot stop them. No matter what pleasure, ecstasy, depression, frustration or guilt I enjoy or suffer, I have to cope with it.

Does it matter that I have this private world? Is it harmful that I should experience this explosion of energy and then have to divert it, resist it, cope with it in any way I can short of fulfilling it with another person? Or would it be more harmful if I were allowed to give full expression to it in any way I could?

There is no area of human experience more confusing and apparently less clearly understood. Throughout history, different communities have devised all manner of policy ranging from total freedom of sexual expression to virtually total suppression. And none have "proved" they have found the "ideal" resolution. Why? Because none have been able to state undeniably and irrefutably *in what interest* such energy should be controlled. Certainly there may be economic considerations—but they are enforced by material circumstances; they have nothing to do with man's possible understanding of the nature of this energy in all its ramifications.

So, until there is such understanding, we are stuck with our particular circumstances. Whatever the dictates and consensus of opinion surrounding us, it is likely that we will find very little in the way of wisdom and reasonable guidance. We will find that there is probably no subject over which adult society, including its religious and secular leadership, is more ignorant, superstitious, prejudiced and uncertain.

And yet, sex energy is the most fundamental force in human experience. The ramifications of it permeate man's every motive and endeavour—including his aesthetic and spiritual aspirations.

Over past centuries, there has often arisen, especially from the religious establishment, much emphasis on the incompatibility of sexuality and spirituality. It has often been propounded that you can indulge in one or the other, but not both. This has tended to establish the idea that material life and religious life are separate.

It is not for us to judge the wisdom of the past—except in so far as it may help us to be wiser now. What is certain is that this dichotomy, this deeply dualistic view, can no longer be maintained if there is to be any improvement in the "health" of modern societies. Sexuality and spirituality may be poles apart—*but poles*

97

are connected. The energy involved is the same energy—the energy of life that informs and enlivens every cell of the body. The more apparently separated the two poles become, the more likely that the intelligence of both will perish.

For, in all its aspects, wisdom about the sexual-spiritual relationship informs everything else—economics, politics, social activities, everything. It is that which conditions man's power—and how he wields it in every field of endeavour. It governs one nation's treatment of another; one person's treatment of another; one person's treatment of himself or herself.

*

Jesus saith unto her (his mother), *Woman, what have I to do with thee? mine hour is not yet come.*

*

And so, in my puberty, I experience the emergence of "life-power".

And, in my innocence and ignorance, I try to cope with it by myself. It is true that from time to time I may find someone to whom I can talk about some aspects—a parent, or a teacher, or an older friend. And such discussion may help me a little. But it will never relieve me fully of the idea that I ought to know and decide for myself how to cope with my own confusion—how to cope with the fact that one part of me feels obliged to resist what another part of me wants to do. I realize that it is up to me; that if there is to be control then it must be "self-control".

What I am not likely to consider is that this duality—the agony and the ecstasy, the desire and its suppression, the love and the hate, and so on—might be a necessary process, in the interest of development and possible transformation.

Does the chick want to burst out of the shell which has been its world and protection? Is the snake worried when it throws off its skin? Does the chrysalis enjoy or suffer the convulsions as it emerges as a butterfly? Did I welcome or resent the trauma of quitting my mother's womb when I was thrust into this world?

98

I wonder?

Perhaps the tensions that I experience as I begin to enjoy and suffer the pleasures and pains of sexual maturity are part of the trauma of a "new birth"—the birth of the new individual, the awakening of a new consciousness, the beginning of the process of transformation, of the conditioned child into the independent adult?

And what energy it is—as I shake off the child that I was and seek to find who I really am! And let us be realistic—it may be a longer process than the world generally recognizes.

*

Sex energy in its broadest sense, as we have suggested, is linked to so many aspects of my behaviour—some of them obvious, some of them less recognizably connected.

I want to succeed. Why? Surely not just for the sake of success—but to impress my friends, my parents, my teachers, and anyone else I want to impress, especially my "hero" or "heroine". Why do I want to impress them? Do I not want to be thought well of? Do I not want—just a little—to be their ideal, to be worshipped, to be admired and loved?

I want, perhaps, to be attractive. I care about my appearance, about my physique and the way I dress. Why? To impress myself? Do I not want to be attractive to other people? After all, it cannot be just for my pleasure because I do not see myself unless I am in front of a mirror! Do I not want—just a little—to be desired?

Or, I want to be and appear intelligent. I care about the statements I make, about how I express my ideas, about how well-informed and knowledgeable I sound. Why? It cannot be simply in order to prove something to myself. Why should I express my ideas, beliefs and opinions if I already know them in my mind? Do I not want—just a little—to be listened to, to be thought wise, to be "inspiring" to other people?

In other words, am I not looking for it to be confirmed that I am "ideal" myself? I want to be perfect, to be whole.

And then, maybe, in this bettering and perfecting, I am increasing

99

the chances of being able to obtain the "ideal" partner—the "god" or "goddess" of my dreams.

*

If, in the days of my emerging sexuality, I am attracted to and admire someone of my own sex, am I not expressing my idea of what I would like to be myself—perhaps being attracted to attributes that I feel I myself lack? And if I am attracted to someone of the opposite sex, am I not expressing my desire for what I feel I need to complement myself, to make me feel complete, whole?

I am ceasing to be a dependent child, relying on my parents, my family, my teachers and my school. I am establishing myself as a "person", the centre of my own individual universe. And here appears to be another fundamental duality.

I am aware that only I can see the secret world inside myself and that I am beginning to have an individual view of the world outside myself. I am alone—as the experiencer of me, and of the world for myself. Apparently, an *inside* world and an *outside* world.

And yet . . . are they separate? How are they related?

*

Alone—inside separated from outside—*lonely*.
All one—no inside *and* outside—*at one*.

*

I seek to find the relationship between myself and the world outside. I need to get from the world outside that which will make me complete inside. That is how I am conditioned to see it.

Is it surprising that I should seek to influence people—and then be annoyed, surprised, disappointed that other people do not necessarily want to see things my way? Is it surprising that I should seek to acquire all kinds of things for myself—and then be frustrated, resentful, disappointed that they do not give me lasting satisfaction?

It seems that *my* way is the only way I can know; it may not occur to me that there are totally different ways of seeing and experiencing.

But, for certain, sooner or later I shall discover that I cannot have it all my own way.

*

The state of physical and mental adolescence becomes one of continual debate—both with myself inside and with others outside.

No longer am I just confused and uncertain within; there seems to be plenty of confusion and uncertainty in the world outside also—and that seems only to make matters worse.

*

People do not always agree with me. And I do not always agree with them. Perhaps, on a point of discussion, I may persuade them my way, or they may persuade me their way.

The point is, I find that for any standpoint or view there is always somewhere *an opposite*—an opposing view. When there is confrontation and both points of view are strongly held, there can only be stalemate; but, if the debate is harmonious and in the interests of further understanding, there may emerge from the two opposing viewpoints an entirely new aspect.

So, in any debate, there are several possibilities.

Perhaps I will be converted to your view.

Perhaps you will be converted to my view.

Perhaps you will reject my view and I will reject yours and we will part unchanged.

Or perhaps our ideas will "marry" and a totally new development will be "born" for both of us—one that we can then both share and be "inspired" by.

This "marriage of true minds" is wonderfully creative. I discover that it removes any sense of separation and loneliness. I am contributing from my view of the world and with my ideas about it, and so are you—and, through our sharing (if the process is being conducted honestly) a wholly new "creation" takes place, a revelation for both of us.

My idea or proposition, your idea or proposition—let us call it "water"—is contained or held by your attention, or my attention—

let us call it "the waterpot"—and is miraculously transformed into a new potential, a new "wine".

*

Let us pause a little further to consider this process of development or transformation.

It seems to come about, is "born", through the active-passive duality.

If both protagonists in the debate hold on to their own ideas positively, then there will only be argument and no development. Similarly, if both are passive and are not interested in the possibility of development, then there will only be idle, discursive chatter or silence; again, no transformation.

But, if one's idea is active and the other is passive-receptive, then there can be the miracle of "marriage-fertilization-birth".

There can be no "fertilization-birth" without there having been "marriage" *first*.

*

Take an ordinary, simple example.

I want to go for a walk with you. You want to play a game of cards with me. We are therefore both positive about what we want to do . . .

I do not mind if we go for a walk or play cards. You do not mind whether we go for a walk or play cards. We are therefore both passive about what we want to do . . .

In either case how can we make a choice?

However, supposing I do not mind what we do and you definitely want to play cards. We play cards! Active desire fires passive receptivity.

So far, so good.

But, is there not also a *third point* that ought to be taken into account?

It is not sufficient that I hold a passive attitude whilst you have an active desire, or *vice versa*. Your desire needs to be reciprocated. In order that the situation may develop, there has to be another,

102

third factor to permit it—an essential, conditioning factor that is often taken for granted and overlooked. In the example above, we need to have the mutual factor that we want to do something with each other—*together*.

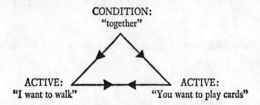

No development!

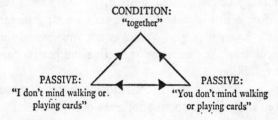

No development!

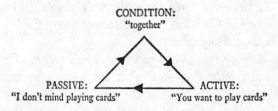

We play cards!

＊

The three forces—active, passive, conditioning—are involved in every situation that is capable of development. It is the relationship between the three—within the trinity—which dictates what happens. When the three interact, there is development or transformation of some kind.

103

If all three are not present, there is impasse, stagnation and gradual deterioration or atrophy.

But, always, it is the conditioning factor that is vital—for the interaction of the other two is random and purposeless without it. There can be no "true marriage" without a conditioning purpose.

*

Jesus saith unto her, Woman, what have I to do with thee? mine hour is not yet come.

*

When the kinetic force penetrates the passive potential, and a third force conditions their meeting, then there is new creation.

A seed may be germinated; a fire may burn; a light bulb may be illuminated; a nail may be knocked into wood; a picture may be painted; a flower may grow; there is not any created thing that is not the result of the "marriage" of active and passive forces within a given condition.

What, I wonder, was the conditioning purpose when "I" was conceived through the coming together of my parents?

*

The Trinity—the three forces in their absolute form—is conceived of by the Christian as the three aspects of God . . .

Father, Son, Holy Ghost.

What do they mean? We can have some notion of Father-Son quality and relationship—but what are we to understand by the mysterious Holy Ghost?

The Creator, the Created—and that which relates them?

*

In the Christian faith-religion, there are four ceremonies in which the Christian, actively or passively, plays his or her role; the *christening*, when the potential individual is admitted to the Christian faith, sponsored by others, and is given a name "in the sight of God"; the *confirmation*, when the emerging, increasingly responsible and conscious individual confirms his allegiance to the faith on his own behalf (and may continue to do so from time to time in the ceremony of *communion* or *the mass*, when the believer reaffirms his kinship with God in the act of coming-into-union through symbolic ritual); the *marriage*, when the mature individual makes a contract with an individual of the opposite sex to complement each other in a partnership "in the sight of God"; and the *funeral*, when the body of the erstwhile incarnate individual is committed to earth or fire and his or her "soul" is released into the "hereafter" where it is hoped it will experience a merciful fate "in God's judgement".

A Christian would expect to go through the first two of these ceremonies in order to be able to call himself "a Christian"; in particular, the confirmation is his active vow of commitment.

The marriage ceremony however is seen as an individual circumstance and is certainly not inevitable. It is not Christian law that you *must* get married; but it is Christian law that if you desire to mate with a person of the opposite sex, and possibly conceive a child through that act, then *first* you must be married within the conditioning context of dedication to "God and his sacred purposes".

What is more, having taken the plunge and mutually agreed to the partnership in front of witnesses, then you must expect to remain together as "man and wife", regardless of any circumstances short of death, for the rest of your lives.

*

What a momentous decision this is for anyone to make!

How can I possibly know *in advance* the full implication of committing myself irrevocably to someone for, maybe, several decades? How can I know that the person to whom I am at the moment attracted and who is apparently attracted to me, is going to remain my desire for the rest of my life? In all matters in my experience so far, I usually do not know what I am going to desire next week, let alone next year . . . but, for the rest of my life? Countless things could happen to either one of us to make us change our minds —and, not only about each other, but about *ourselves*.

How many of the things that you desperately desired and found so important five years ago are desired and highly valued now?

In the first place, one inevitable fact is that we will both grow older. Physically, we will change enormously; what happens if we cease to be attractive to each other?

And, in the second place, and far more important than physical change, we will alter mentally. All well and good if it is a mutual development, each changing in harmony with the other, refining and re-defining our ideas, ideals, goals, beliefs, attitudes, both altering compatibly through shared experience, maturing through a linked transformation . . . all well and good indeed . . .

But, again, how can I possibly assess in advance the chances of the marriage succeeding in these respects?

And, if it does not, what are the alternatives?

If we continue, obedient to our vows, to be "man and wife", there are two possibilities; either the partnership will cease to evolve, stagnating in a day-to-day existence occupied with repetitive ritual and habit, seeking escapes and entertainments, failing to explore or question, either because the inspiration has atrophied or fearful that for one to do so without the other would place unbearable strain on the remaining bond; or we shall go our separate ways, regardless of each other, each getting on with his or her life—two "strangers", with no "third point" to unite them any more, just the memory of a ceremonial vow made many years ago, an array of mutual possessions and perhaps some offspring which we may claim to be "ours".

Why, one might wonder, did the marriage vows ever come into existence?

Were they necessary in the first primitive societies in order to encourage and persuade parents to be responsible for their children?

Or, did they evolve out of religious thought—so that the enigma of birth might be properly "sanctified" and so that a deeper understanding of the parental role might be instilled into the sweeping passion of sexual appetite?

Or was it, again, in the interests of law and order, the smooth running of the group? By giving their word in public, at a specially convened and elaborately celebrated ritual, to be faithful to each other, there would be less disorder, dissension and rivalry resulting from undisciplined promiscuity?

There will be many reasons—but they are all to do with discipline. Somehow the energy of sexual desire must not be allowed to run riot but must be controlled, directed, sublimated and perhaps transformed—hopefully to the benefit of the society and the individual.

*

The institution of marriage as a religious ceremony—and the associated dictates influencing sexual behaviour—is increasingly challenged today (as the two poles, sexuality-spirituality, apparently move further apart). The Christian Church is racked by bitter debate—both within its own hierarchy of officials and among its followers at large—as it tries to reconcile opposing factions and take a unified stance on such matters as pre-marital sex, common-law marriage, divorce, birth control, abortion, female priests, euthanasia, and so on.

Undoubtedly, over the ages and over one issue or another, the Church has frequently been challenged. But perhaps, in its many faceted and wide-sweeping problems, the turmoil of today is worse than it has ever been. The trouble seems to be a lack of inspired and recognized authority. Authority depends upon either force or knowledge; the former is out of the question and the latter seems lacking.

But, as we have suggested earlier, perhaps it is this very turmoil that will produce the inspiration for a new dispensation, the birth of a new era in human history. That so many are now "thinking for themselves" and challenging materialist ideologies, superstition and dogma—whilst others are resorting to increasingly extreme and violent standpoints—may well be the prelude to such a development.

*

One aspect of the fundamental question, "What is the relationship between sexuality and spirituality?" is the experience of the phenomenon that we call "love".

What is the relationship between physical "love", mental "love" and spiritual "love"?

Must they not be intimately linked?

It is surely no coincidence that the sexual energy emerging at puberty and the "religious awakening" at the time of confirmation coincide.

*

"Love", as I first experience it, and try to understand it, brings close on its heels its complement "hate".

Love and hate—again I am faced with the deep duality of attraction-repulsion, unifying and separating.

It seems sometimes that my entire life is made up of divisive dualities—and that the tension created between them somehow generates the energies which drive me through life, making endless choices and decisions.

And the Christian tradition has a classic, dualistic goal to offer me as I go along—one which seems to symbolize all the opposing poles in my life: *heaven* and *hell*.

The former is a realm of peace, bliss and fulfilment—if I obey the laws of "god"; the latter is a realm of torment and suffering, if I disobey.

So, where can the "third point" be between heaven and hell? The condition of "me" here on earth?

And where is the "third point" between loving and hating?

Am I not it?

And can I not experience *my* heaven here and now—not later after *my* death? Anyone who has experienced the bliss of love must recognize that.

And can I not experience *my* hell here and now—not later after *my* death. Anyone who has experienced the anguish, disillusionment and depression of being "out of love" must recognize that.

I must be the third point; for *I* am the one who witnesses the experience of heaven and hell.

Could there be heaven and hell, love and hate, unifying and separating, oneness and loneliness, if *I* did not observe them?

*

When do I marry—in the sense of coming to love that from which I now think myself separate?

"Marriage" is now such a debased word. Can we not "marry" in mind, in thought, in idea—and not just in body?

So when do I marry in this sense?

When I first meet another person—or when I first "espouse" another person's idea/dream/inspiration?

When I go through a ceremony of avowal to partner another person—or ideal?

When I first make love with that partner?

When I first conceive with that partner?

Who am I marrying? What marries what?

There is you and there is me—"based" on two separate bodies.

I observe that "things" happen to me and I observe that "things" happen to you.

What is the third point between you and me?

I think "I am"; you think "I am"; we both think "I am".

Is that not so? *I* am. Therein we are married.

Is there a difference between the two "I's"—your "I" and my "I", the one unknown to you, the other unknown to me?

"Who am I?" I ask. "Who am I?" you ask.

Could it be that we are both speaking of the same "I"?

Our bodies "marry"; our minds "marry"; but can "I" marry unless it be that "I" cease to become "separate" from anything and everything?

Could it be that contracting to "marry" has little to do with the common and limited connotation of the word?

Could it be that "marriage" has to do with dedication by you and me to becoming unified, becoming "whole", knowing "who *I* am"?

*

Together, we may atone for the failure in each other.

Atone.

At-one.

*

If both of us are "called" or compelled to know and understand the real *I*—to know "who *I* am"—and if both of us are aware that no one can give us the answers to our deepest questions, that only *I* can do that, then our "marriage" will be blessed indeed and certainly "in the sight of God". For neither of us will interfere with the other's quest, neither will attempt to hold the other back, neither will attempt to influence the other against their will. Instead, we will mutually support each other as we make our way deeper into the labyrinth that is the spiritual quest. Together, we may provide the active-passive duality, "working" in an ever-changing pattern or dance, constantly linked by the "third point", the real "*I*" that is at the heart of both of us.

You and me—we will be married "*in* Christ".

What have such things to do with my desiring *you* and you desiring *me*?

And, of course, we shall be responsible for our "offspring".

My desires and your desires are as fleeting and as changing as the seasons of the year or the days of the week. There can be no trusting in their constancy—paradoxically, we can only be sure of their inconstancy.

Only *I* am constant ("standing with"), the central witness of everything that happens whilst there is life in this body.

*

And the third day there was a marriage in Cana of Galilee . . .

The *third* day.

The *third* point?

*

The marriage in Cana—a factual story about the once-and-for-all ceremony that human beings commit themselves to? A badly-prepared feast where the wine ran out prematurely, or where the guests were drinking a lot more wine than they were expected to, and where there was only water left when it came to toasting the bride and groom?

Or a symbolic story about "true marriage", a continuing contract in life where two bodies and two minds unite to resolve conflicting duality in the miracle of atonement and transformation?

*

Every man at the beginning doth set forth good wine; and when men have well drunk, then that which is worse: but thou hast kept the good wine until now.

*

Every vow to marry, except the rare few, is contracted in the full sweep of emotional love. But, how is it that I can love today—and possibly hate tomorrow?

How can I hate that which I once loved?

What has changed? The object of the love; or me; or both?

Me, the inconsistent and wayward performer in life, mistakes the desire to possess for love and obscures the reality—that "I am in love" always. And "being in love" *I* can work "miracles", for *I* am always present at the continuing "marriage" of dualities that is called life.

*

Marriage, as a religious or civil institution, is threatened in the world today. More and more people are living together and bearing children without first going through any form of ceremonial commitment. "What," they may say, "is the point of a ceremony if we do not believe in it?" Fair enough—providing their not making an "official" commitment to each other does not mean that they are unwilling to make any "sacrifice" to each other.

For the greater ceremony, unknown to the world, is what *I* promise to myself—what vow I make to myself. And then, whether I am able to keep it, or whether I betray it and realize the consequences.

If I allow you your freedom to develop . . . if you allow me mine . . . if I support you when you fail . . . and you look for me when

I am lost . . . if we remind each other that at heart we are the same—not by telling but by seeing ourselves reflected in each other's eyes . . .

"Miracle" comes from the same root as "mirror", meaning "look at". When we reflect each other, then we will be married indeed, moment to moment. For each will be wholly apart and yet wholly together. Through seeing, knowing and understanding "our reflections of ourselves", we may become unified, "whole". We will have invoked the "spirit", the ingredient which distinguishes "wine" from "water".

*

This beginning of miracles did Jesus in Cana of Galilee, and manifested forth his glory; and his disciples believed on him.

*

Did Jesus really turn water into wine?

In this age of scientific fact and law, it sounds a remarkable feat. But then, do I understand "miracle" correctly? I tend to think of it as a marvellous, mysterious, extraordinary event brought about by some supernatural agency. But that is only a vague definition or explanation—I do not really know what it means.

On the other hand, I tend to take for granted and think ordinary a thousand thousand things which I also do not really understand, no matter how advanced my learning of the scientific facts.

I do not *know* how a blade of grass grows—how it *knows* how to grow. I do not know how a bird knows its song. I do not know how a plant knows how to blossom into flower. I do not know how I think, what life is, how my brain gives me a sense of myself . . . The deeper I penetrate into the labyrinth, I begin to realize that I do not *really know* anything at all. I have only learned an array of superficial explanations, collected a mass of assumptions.

And the deeper I go, the more anything and everything seems to be a "miracle" . . . the very fact that I breathe, that I am writing on this page . . . it is all one colossal, mysterious and glorious miracle.

In the Gospels I discover that Jesus is reported to have performed many miracles: he made the blind see; he made the lame walk; he made the sick healthy . . .

Perhaps he really did such things—I do not know. Today, doctors make the lame walk, make the blind see, make the sick healthy, so . . .

If I involve myself too much in the factual elements of the historical report, I become lost, and reach a point which demands that I must simply "believe".

On the other hand, without dismissing the possibility of a man with supernatural powers, the miracles of Jesus may be of value to me as metaphors and symbols. And if I find them valuable as such, and they inspire my experience of life now, is there any reason why I should not glean such value? May it not be that their extraordinary strength lies in their ability to inspire and illuminate in many ways at many levels? Is that not what religion is supposed to do?

If, through the teachings of wise men, I realize that in my view of life, in my behaviour, in my thinking and beliefs, I have been, as it were, blind, lame, sick . . .

*

All the miracles in the Christ story point in one direction—being transformed, being made "whole".

And the greatest miracle of all was to do with the "overcoming" of death or being "raised to eternal life". Jesus raised the "dead" during his ministry, but he reserved the ultimate enactment of this miracle for his own "death". And so it must be for us—the ultimate miracle.

It seems strangely fitting that the first miracle of transformation should have been at a marriage, a wedding feast, where water was made into wine.

*

Jesus said: Many are standing at the door, but the solitary are the ones who will enter the bridal chamber.

(Thomas, Log. 75)

Eight

Conception—a third body is originated from the "marriage" of two other bodies.

Birth—the new body is mature enough to become an independent entity. A new "mind" originates, "innocent" and "virgin", and begins to experience the outside world, and to memorize what it learns.

Baptism—the life of the new being is dedicated by others to Christianity, a "philosophy of life" pronounced historically by Jesus of Nazareth, two thousand years ago. The child is given a name.

Childhood—the body grows and matures further. The mind is conditioned with all manner of learning and "me", the ego or personality, develops.

Puberty—as sex energy emerges, the body becomes mature enough to be able to reproduce the species. Personality is now established in mind and is "stamped" on the body (in walk, posture, facial expression, etc.) The independent person begins to evolve as "I" awareness, self-consciousness, increases. "I am born" and the spiritual life, the search for truth, begins.

Confirmation—the individual confirms dedication to the Christian concept of God and the religious life as exemplified by Jesus Christ.

Adolescence—the body reaches full maturity; mind continues to mature, experiencing duality, particularly the "pull" of the senses towards desires and sexuality, and, the apparent opposite, the "call" that appeals to the "higher nature" of man, to cultural and aesthetic development, to the search for truth and the religious ideals of service, to others and to God.

Adulthood—playing a part in society. The friction caused by the apparent duality of what "me" wants to do and what "me" ought to do. The possibility of spiritual maturity, of the real "I" transcending all conditioned dualities and divisions, governing the mind and body, of becoming "whole"—as opposed to the chaos of "soul-destroying", selfish, conflicting desires which give rise to the many "me"s, dividing, separating, distracting and disturbing the mind.

Marriage—one "half" of a duality being complemented by the other "half"; the resolution of dualities, physical and mental, giving rise to a new "being"; the impotent "water" of "my" inadequacy is turned into the "wine of love", the unifying spirit; coming to be "in love" with all and everything, the creator being re-united with the creation through the mind of man.

Death—either destruction or completion, disintegration of the body, disbanding of the mind, release (or realizing) of the real "I", the Son re-united with the Father.

*

. . . And they took Jesus, and led him away.

And he bearing his cross went forth into a place called the place of a skull, which is called in the Hebrew Golgotha:

Where they crucified him, and two other with him, on either side one, and Jesus in the midst.

(John, 19:16–18)

*

Because for most of my life I do not know how or when I will die, my death and its implications are not something that I think about very much.

I may have a rough idea when it *should* be—in my old age—but even that is only an approximation.

With the advance of medical science and general living standards, the span of human life has, on average, increased over recent decades. There was a time, I am told, when very few people lived into their seventies; but now, in the technologically advanced countries, most people would hope to live into their eighties or even nineties.

So, for the majority of my active life, death is an event that I can ignore. "I'll think about it later," I may say to myself, "when I am old . . . "

However, for all the expectation of longer life in these modern times, there is a host of hazards that may dash my hopes of a "natural" death—simply running down and stopping.

I could die tomorrow . . . or even today.

The ceiling could fall on my head at this very moment; I could be run over in the street; I could burn, drown, be poisoned . . . all manner of "accidental" death could strike.

Or I could fall victim of disease; or suffer a fatal illness, dying of "ill-health" or malfunction of a vital organ or system.

Perhaps I am unwise to postpone consideration of my death—for I have no idea how imminent it may be and I would prefer to be prepared for it.

Why?

Because, given the opportunity, I know instinctively that it is very important to try to understand how to meet it.

*

There is a game that is sometimes played.

It is simply a question to which you have to supply an answer.

"If you knew that you were going to die next week, how would you spend that week?"

It has been said that such a situation "concentrates the mind wonderfully". The answers that I come up with can be very revealing about *me*, especially about how my life is motivated.

Would I immediately take whatever money I have and spend it doing as many as possible of the things I have always wanted to do?

Would I go somewhere with the person I love most dearly and spend every possible moment in their company?

Would I work very hard to finish some important project or business that I am engaged upon?

Would I, in short, try to make up for lost time, enjoying myself, trying to get the most of what the world has to offer?

Or would I suddenly try to piece together all the hints and assurances that religion has to offer about "life after death"?

Or would I hope that someone could give me something—maybe a drug—which would allow me to escape the issue and sink into oblivion?

I suppose that my answer would depend on the sort of person I am—how afraid I am of dying and how I have evaluated and spent my life.

Am I afraid of death?

How do I prepare for it?

*

Do I love life?

Sometimes, yes I do, very much.

When things are going well for me; when I am loved and in love; when I am happy and contented with my circumstances; when I am satisfying my desires, having my wishes granted, achieving my ambitions; then the world seems a good place and my life is happy and fulfilling. Who would gladly give up such an enjoyable state? Certainly I do not want to die. "Life is good," I say, "I love life."

But what about those times when nothing seems to be going right? My hopes are dashed, my desires frustrated, my wishes denied, my love betrayed, my ambitions fail, I suffer pain and anguish—do I love life then? "Life is hell," I say, "I would rather be dead."

Would I? Do I really mean that? Is the best way to meet death to be in a state when I do not want to go on living?

Presumably, in order to be able to say that life is hell, I must have experienced life as heaven? I cannot judge the one unless I can compare it with the other—relative to my own experience of course for no one can experience the quality and degree of someone else's heaven or hell.

If life had *always* been hell, I would not expect it to be any other way; I would simply accept that that was how it was.

So, how seriously do I ever wish to be dead? When I experience life as hell, I always hope that it will improve again and, if I can,

I try to change the oppressive circumstances, search for alleviation, and look to retrieving a state nearer to my idea of heaven.

*

Yes, there is the possibility that the circumstances are so bad that there is no hope—and then there is suicide. Suicide is a cardinal sin in the Christian ethic. Usually, this ultimate act is judged to take place when "the balance of mind is disturbed".

It would seem that committing suicide is a sin because it is killing yourself without just cause. It is all right to "commit suicide" by volunteering to fight for your country and getting yourself killed in the field of battle. It is all right to kill yourself saving the life of someone else.

And if we are to believe the Christ story literally, we must assume that he had just cause for killing himself, for we cannot avoid the fact that he deliberately brought death upon himself. He evidently knew that his life was threatened by his actions; he made no attempt to avert a sequence of events of which the climax was predictable; in fact, in several respects, he actively assisted by directing others to play their parts to ensure that he would be put to death.

For what reason? "That we might be saved."

How am I possibly to understand that?

How could someone who deliberately engineered his own death two thousand years ago possibly "save" me today?

It is reported that after being crucified to death, "he arose again from the dead."

How am I possibly to understand that?

Does it mean that if I "follow him"—deliberately bringing about my own death—I will also "rise from the dead"?

I cannot, at the moment, when I assume that my balance of mind is not disturbed, easily contemplate the idea of "committing suicide" —for whatever good reason—perhaps least of all on the basis that, if I believe the Christ story, I *might* "rise again".

But, perhaps, this is the wrong way of trying to understand it?

Perhaps, again, we have here a deeply significant, symbolic story?

*

I desire to live, and go on living as long as possible—naturally.
But, if my reasoning so far is valid, the worth of my life has got little
or nothing to do with how many years I manage to complete, how
much wealth, happiness, fame I manage to obtain, the amount of
pleasure I manage to cram in, the amount of knowledge or skill I
manage to acquire—it has to do essentially with *how* I live it.

*

How I live my life has everything to do with its quality—and
nothing to do with its quantity—how it can be measured in the
world's terms.

And the more I ponder on the quality of my life—trying to give
value to what I say and do—the more I become aware of the debate
inside myself, the conflict between the opposing "voices", the wear
and tear of choosing and deciding between alternative views, the
confusion of the meaning of "good" and "bad", the distinction
between really knowing and false justification and explanation, the
seeing clearly what is imaginary and what real, what is subjective and
what objective, what is sense and what is nonsense . . . a catalogue
of bewildering and sometimes paralysing controversy inside myself.

And this process in my mind manifests in my speech and actions.
And I notice that beliefs and opinions change; and according to
the strength of a desire in a given moment, so my behaviour is
dictated. I become aware that this person that I call "me", whom
I like to believe to be a cohesive entity, is many-sided and frequently
inconsistent, inconstant, contradictory, the master of compromise
and excuse—anything but well-directed and whole.

All the different bits of my personality—what I may call all the
different "me"s—take it in turn to speak and initiate action in my
name. They all claim to be "I"; and the mind goes to considerable
pains to maintain a coherent image of this "I".

If I really want the truth, if I really want to know who I am and
I am prepared to admit my deception, this is the point where I

must give account and explore the labyrinth to find out what is going on!

*

Where are the desires and motives experienced?
In the body or in the mind?
Are the body and the mind separate?
Would the desires and the motives exist if I did not experience them?
Where is the "I" which experiences them?
What am I to my body and my mind?
Are they three separate "things"?
Am I not that which witnesses both body and mind?
It may not be correct—indeed, it is certainly an over-simplification—but let us, since this view is common experience, consider this trinity of factors.

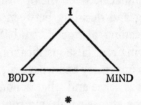

*

As a result of the many and varied interactions of these three factors—according to what is happening in the body and what is arising in the mind—there takes place the experience, speech and action that is believed to be "me" and "mine".

Basically, in my judgement and in the eyes of the world, there are two types of "me"—the "good" and the "bad".

*

... and two other with him, on either side one ...

*

The "I", the single essence of the being that "I am", "enters" and is present, when "I am conscious of myself".

When "I am", I witness all the experiences of my mind and body.

120

"I" am here, in existence, as long as there are a mind and a body to be aware of.

And "I" am the witness of the good "me"s and the bad "me"s—the product of the desires that compete in my mind. However the world may judge the words spoken and the actions performed in my name, I am the one who must judge for myself which is the "good" and which is the "bad"—inasmuch as either may deceive they may both be cause of illness. (A malefactor is one who "makes ill").

*

The single, most powerful image of the Christian faith has come to be the cross. It is commonly in the place of honour, on the altar, in Christian churches. As a *symbol*, it is worshipped and revered.

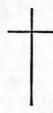

This emblem has become the focus of Christian worship and perhaps we could say that it represents the very essence of the teachings and deeds of the man called Jesus Christ.

A Christian will tell me—or I may read of it in the Gospels—that the original cross was a wooden structure on which Jesus was crucified and died, with nails through his hands and his feet.

Indeed, very often, the replicas of the original cross bear an effigy of a man—outstretched, pinned to the upright and crossbar, suffering the severest agony as the nails tear the flesh and the blood spills from a wound in his side.

It is the most barbaric and cruel image.

Is this really the central feature, the focus, for the worship of hundreds of millions of Christians?

How does this extraordinary execution-cum-"suicide" take away "the sins of the world"?

As a factual history, the crucifixion seems the most terrible example of man's inhumanity to man. How does it come about that a large section of human society should revere such an incident whilst the consensus of opinion in civilized society today condemns capital punishment as abhorrent?

And why, whilst we are questioning, should Judas Iscariot, who is supposed to have "betrayed" Jesus, be so reviled in the eyes of the world when it is evident from the Gospels that Jesus *told* him to do it? How could the story have been fulfilled without him?

*

On a literal level, we are faced with a maze of facts which are bewildering—apparently perversely so—for an innocent, honest and sincere aspirant who simply wants to know the truth, simply wants to live the best possible life, if only someone will just explain straightforwardly what is to be done.

Why should it be so complicated?

After all the divisions of opinion, all the theological debate, all the confusing statements and counter-statements, the claims and the counter-claims, are we ever likely to untangle the truth?

*

But, supposing again, it is a symbolic story.

Among the many clues, let us take just one.

Why, I wonder, do three of the four Gospels think it important to mention that the crucifixion was enacted at *a place called the place of a skull* . . .

Why the emphasis on "skull"?

*

Where do all my desires, my wishes, my beliefs, my conflicts of choice and decision, and the awareness "I am", manifest themselves?

In my "mind"?

Where is my mind?

In my brain?

Where is my brain?

In my skull.

*

In an earlier chapter, we touched on the story of the temptation of Jesus by the devil in the wilderness.

Where did the devil take Jesus?

Into the "holy city", to a "pinnacle of the temple".

The body is often referred to in the scriptures as the "temple". Where could the pinnacle be but high in the skull?

"Temple" means "a part cut off" or "a place from which one can survey". Perhaps this suggests the place where "I am"—the one "I" or "eye"—above the two eyes and the two temples?

"Temple" is also related to "time"; perhaps the "pinnacle of the temple" is the ultimate "point" of time—now?

*

There are many other clues when once you begin to look in this way. But, we must ask, is this symbolic approach valid?

It depends whether it is meaningful—whether the mind responds to it and recognizes the meaning in its own experience.

Does it seem reasonable?

If I begin to see unfolding an illuminating picture of my own state . . . then will I not understand?

*

When I survey the experience of living, I see it full of desires which I think are related to the likelihood or otherwise of my achieving happiness.

I can see that my unhappiness stems apparently from my not having my desires, wishes, hopes and ambitions fulfilled.

And I base that on the fact that my happiness in life appears to have resulted from the pleasure of having desires, wishes, hopes and ambitions gratified.

But is that really true?

When my worldly desires are gratified, do they not immediately spawn further desires, fears and doubts? If I achieve a degree of wealth, possession, fame and power, knowledge and success, do I rest content?

Can that elusive and transitory pleasure be real happiness?

How, for example, does the fleeting pleasure of desire gratified compare with the happiness when "taken out of myself", of being "in love", of being wholly at peace—in the desireless state of mind where there are no conflicting dualities?

*

I appear to have a choice—between involvement in pursuit of the desires of the world and forsaking such pursuit.

Do I want to go on being pulled hither and thither, rising and falling, happy one moment, miserable the next. Or do I want to grow in understanding, gain in strength, little by little discovering the key to the permanent states of love, peace and harmony.

By this choice, I am transfixed on the "cross" of duality.

(And all men, whether they realize it or not, are on it also.)

I came, at the beginning, into my body, into my mind, into the realm of desire, into the world. To decide to forsake this world, to "die" to it, is a deliberate "suicide", a betrayal (which means "giving over"). It is a surrender of self-will; and there are stages of that surrender.

So, in my mind, I can see that crucifixion represents my state—my body in and of the earth, my mind divided "right" and "left" (the "good" me and the "bad" me being crucified at the same time) and, at the top of the central pillar (in my skull), the real "I" prepared to "sacrifice" itself in order that it might be re-united with the cause of itself—God.

*

There is an alternative to this surrender—its opposite.

I might decide to take control of my mind and body through an exceptional effort of will, exceptional discipline and an obsessive desire for power.

That is dangerous.

For what would I do with that power?

Apply it to the fulfilment of my desires, wishes and ambitions?

Then indeed may the devil be said to be tempting me!

*

But, can I live without ambitions? How can I work and contribute to the welfare of the community if I do not want to succeed in achieving?

Perhaps the best work I ever do, or will ever do, is that which is not done in response to my desire to gain for myself but is done in response to the needs of others? Maybe I will notice a quite different sense of satisfaction and enjoyment in a task performed for its own sake, when I am not concerned how the results will affect me?

How will I ever go anywhere, or do anything, if I do not have the desire to do so?

Again, it is a question of evaluating the motive or feeling accompanying the prompting to go somewhere or do something. Am I driven to take action because of an immoderate desire to gain something, to indulge excessively, maybe directly or indirectly at the expense of someone else? Again, perhaps, it is a case of being moved by what needs to be done, as it presents itself to me from time to time?

How can I extend myself or improve the lot of my family, say, if I do not pursue the "things" of the world?

Do I *know* how I need to be extended? If there is to be any real worth in the efforts I must make, must they not be in response to demands and needs from outside myself? Beyond the basic requirements of the family for shelter, clothing, food—the essentials—do I *know* what the members of the family need? Must I not respond to the needs as and when they arise?

I respond to *known* need—not desires based on illusions and imaginings.

*

And so, I move a little closer to discovering the "religious" life, knowing *how* to live, gaining a sense of value.

I enjoy what is there—not desire what is not there.

Of course, that is easier said than done. There are many years of conditioning and habit well established in my mind; it will take considerable time to remove the influence of false belief, assumption and superstition.

It will not be a case of just a single "crucifixion"; it will be a continuing process, with different phases and degrees of realization, right through a lifetime.

※

For whosoever hath, to him shall be given, and he shall have more abundance: but whosoever hath not, from him shall be taken away even that he hath.

(Matthew, 13:12)

※

In Arabic, the word "sin" means "moon".

How strange that we should have borrowed that precise word and should have given it such different meaning in the English language. Or is it so different?

In the dark night sky, the moon shines, bright with light. No one can deny that.

But the moon has no light of its own; it simply reflects the light of the sun.

I wonder what my desires, my wishes and my ambitions *are*? I wonder where they come from? Perhaps, in themselves, they are not "bad" at all? Perhaps they are the reflections of what I am really after?

Perhaps the "sin" is the falling into the deceptive belief that they are the source of the light—the source of happiness—and not remembering or knowing that they are but a pale reflection of the light of the sun—the real source—which at night we cannot even see.

"Sinning" is thus "mistaking" illusion for reality.

※

And the light shineth in darkness; and the darkness comprehended it not.

※

Can *I* sin?

Do *I* mistake the reflection of myself for the reality?

※

Jesus said: When you make the two one, you shall become sons of Man, and when you say: "Mountain, be moved", it will be moved.

(Thomas, Log. 106)

126

Nine

*But Thomas, one of the twelve, called Didymus, was not with them
when Jesus came.*

*The other disciples therefore said unto him, We have seen the
Lord. But he said unto them, Except I shall see in his hands the print
of the nails, and put my finger into the print of the nails, and thrust
my hand into his side, I will not believe.*

*And after eight days again his disciples were within, and Thomas
with them: then came Jesus, the doors being shut, and stood in the
midst, and said, Peace be unto you.*

*Then saith he to Thomas, Reach hither thy finger, and behold my
hands; and reach hither thy hand, and thrust it into my side: and
be not faithless, but believing.*

And Thomas answered and said unto him, My Lord and my God.

*Jesus saith unto him, Thomas, because thou hast seen me, thou hast
believed: blessed are they that have not seen, and yet have believed.*

(John, 20:24–29)

*

During my journey through life, I can ignore traditional religion
—the established religious structure. I can avoid committing myself
to Christianity—or any other form of religion.

If such questions arise, I do not have to try to answer "Who am
I?", "What am I here for?", "What happens when I die?" and so
on. I can believe what it suits me to believe; and I can doubt what
it suits me to doubt. Even under the most autocratic and restrictive
of political regimes, I am free to believe and doubt—providing I
do not express myself in opposition to the official ideology. Ultimately, I am only answerable to myself for what goes on in my

mind. Other people may benefit or suffer through what I say and do but—and rarely is this taken into account—I, and only I, am *bound* to suffer through what goes on in my mind.

*

What is "believing"?

One way of considering it is that it is the mind thinking and accepting that it knows the truth about something. Supposing you have, when your mind starts to work as a child, an infinite capacity to believe. Every time you commit yourself to a belief, you surrender part of that limitless capacity; in other words, it is in fact no longer limitless. It is as though you have given something of yourself away. And, immediately you believe something, you admit the possibility of having to deny that which threatens or contradicts the verity of the belief you have adopted. You have lost the "virginity" of your mind.

On the other hand, supposing you believed everything? You would most likely be judged at best naive, at worst a fool.

Why does there have to be believing and disbelieving?

You believe something when you believe it to be true; and disbelieve what you think or feel is untrue.

Yet do we ever really *know* the truth about anything—the whole truth?

Why do we have to surrender the pure and innocent state of just being to what we think is true?

*

Verily I say unto you, Whosoever shall not receive the kingdom of God as a little child shall in no wise enter therein.

(Luke, 18:17)

*

Anyone can avoid the traditional forms of religion; but they have to have *a* religion—a set of rules by which to conduct themselves. It may be going a bit far to grace it with the label "a philosophy of life" but, no matter how crude and little thought out, everyone has to have one.

128

But how *deeply* do I believe mine? It is one which in the main has been arbitrarily selected from my personal experience within a system that has been imposed on me throughout my education. Just how comprehensive and effective is it? Just enough to get by from day to day?

Firstly, I believed those things that I acquired in my childhood— those ideas, beliefs, attitudes, opinions, passed on to me by my parents, my family, my school, my tribe—and which became so embedded in my make-up so long ago that they continually and automatically condition my thinking. They are such "permanent fixtures" that I hardly realize they are there; I even assume that some of them are general and indisputable. I have adopted them and subscribe to them as if they were absolute criteria.

And then I have assumed certain beliefs about myself. How I came to believe these things is rather more subtle. Nevertheless, I think I know the sort of person I am—with my abilities and limitations, my likes and dislikes, my personal idiosyncrasies. These again are beliefs that I rarely question once they are established— even if I am sometimes surprised by what other people think I am like! Whatever attributes I think I have—both "good" and "bad" —I nevertheless claim them and maintain them because they are "me". I have to have them it seems, otherwise people would not recognize me; I would not have an identity without them.

Then there is another set of assumed beliefs. I believe that I know —or should know—what I want to be, what I want to do in life, what I want to possess, what I want to achieve. These may not be so clearly defined or established in my mind—but I do tend to believe that such matters are my choice because, fundamentally I have assumed and believe that it is *my* life.

In just these few examples of belief, I can see that I think and behave to a large extent like a programmed machine. I seem to have been conditioned to such a degree that I have little room left for manoeuvre—although, again, I am still prepared to believe that I have free will.

*

All this learning and belief that has been indoctrinated into my mind seems to satisfy what we may call the functional, logical level of my thinking. This pragmatic information is endorsed usually by the evidence of the senses, the law of cause and effect, and is manifestly credible. For instance, if I put my hand into fire, it will burn.

And this "method" of thinking projects its way into subtler levels. If I break the law, I will be punished; if I attempt something that I do not think myself capable of accomplishing, I will be frustrated and will fail; if life does not work out well according to my ideas as to how it should be, I will be unhappy; if I earn enough money, I will be able to buy all the things that will make life worthwhile. Thus I learn to believe that certain results are inevitable given certain circumstances—and I think dualistically, assessing the pros and cons, the either-or, the yes-and-no, the this and therefore that.

*

This self-centred and limited situation—layer upon layer and horizon upon horizon of "closed-circuit" alternatives and choices—is a life-style that will apparently encompass me from cradle to grave. And yet, curiously, I am loath to surrender it and, perhaps, even loath to question it. It is tightly bound up with what I think I am and it seems to be all there is. What is more, it comes to have the security of familiarity.

If I stand aside from it for a moment, and *look* and *listen*, then I may sense the limit of "my little world". I may sense that in hanging on to it I am denying the possibility of a far greater understanding. But I prefer to believe the familiar—that which I can "touch". I doubt whether I can abandon it; I am afraid of the possible implications.

If these beliefs, all that I have to support me, prove primitive and ill-founded . . . ? If I have "built my house on foundations of sand" . . . ? Where will I be able to turn for comfort and reassurance? Who will be able to help me?

The trouble is, I have also believed in death. If the end of everything is to be the strange, mysterious enigma through which I am annihilated, how should I conduct myself? If, whatever I do, I end up dead, sooner or later, does it matter a scrap what I believe? It is a baffling dilemma.

It is the death of "me" that paralyses my spirit and seems to be a constant threat to my so-called "sanity", to the logical workings of my mind, to the security of my beliefs—no matter how "holy" they are.

Yet, supposing . . . supposing the "blind", ill-considered beliefs I hold are not at all "sane" (healthy) but are decidedly "mad"? Supposing the beliefs, assumptions and opinions that I hold are like "demons" which "possess" my mind?

Supposing . . . above all . . . supposing I see that it is utterly absurd to claim this living as *my* life? I may have it at the moment but what reason have I to believe that it has been given to me to keep for my own use? If it were *really* mine, as opposed to having been "lent" to me, it could not be taken from me. Whose is it to give and to take away? Mine?

Supposing I see this clearly and I realize that I must give up the misguided claim to this life being "mine", will I then not also "give *it* up" (and thereby possibly "save" it)?

If, in this life, I am continually "crucified" by duality, all of which arises from desires in my mind, I can at any moment "surrender" my will. I will have to forsake the pursuits of the world in the sense that I will no longer look to them as a possible source of lasting happiness and fulfilment; I will have to "die" to selfish gratification.

And this will be done through realization of the illusion or delusion of my thinking—not through a desire to "escape" responsibility, or through bitterness or resentment, or through anger at the folly of my beliefs and wayward desires (" . . . they know not what they do . . . "). It will be done through "love of truth".

*

But . . . to what do I surrender and give up "my" life?

*

It is possible—and I have to "admit" this possibility—that through study of the Christ story, of the Christ teaching and life, I may realize that I must abandon many of the habitual ideas, beliefs and opinions that I have about myself and about the world in which I find myself. In the process I may come to respect Christ and to love "him" as the supreme symbol of the truth. I may come to see that I carry my cross from the cradle to the grave and I may accept, through the Christ example, that sooner or later I must give up a fundamental belief—that it is "my" life.

And, if there is to be a "resurrection" and if there is to be an "ascension", they will not be for the "me" I think I am and will not be understood by the ordinary workings of the mind.

For as long as *I am* in this body and claim it as mine, and for as long as *I am* of this mind and claim its contents as mine, then I will continue to experience the world through the particular laws to which they are subject. It cannot be otherwise.

But, if I give them up, I may experience "another world" where there are different laws (of space, time, consciousness and matter), a world and life "hereafter".

*

It is here—in our exploration of the labyrinth of the mind—that we enter the "mysteries". We come to the end of logical, scientific explanation in the terms of "this world" and are on the threshold of "mystical experience".

Such experiences could be called "psychological phenomena" if we have to give them a label at all; with the best of intentions (and for as many who would like to believe in such experiences there seem to be as many who are determined to disprove them), the scientist and the psychologist cannot "explain" and make them "ordinary" with logic and fact. A "mystery" cannot, by definition, be explained. And, since these experiences are not "of this world", it is not surprising that they cannot be understood in the terms of this world. And, for the same reason, those who do experience them have considerable difficulty in describing them.

The scriptures of the religious traditions carry much evidence of the extra-ordinary states of mind called, in the most general term, "mystical". This evidence is sometimes well masked by historical narrative, parable and allegory, and sometimes it is obvious, even if highly symbolic. The Christian tradition, for example, had many notable mystics in the Middle Ages in Europe, and, in the accepted canon of the Bible, the Book of Revelation is a remarkable example. And frequently in the Gospels, especially according to St. John and Thomas, intimations of truth transcending duality are given in enigmatic and illogical statements which baffle ordinary thinking.

We cannot embark here on a study of mysticism. It will be sufficient to recognize that there are realms or states of mind described which indicate "other worlds" and "life hereafter". And, further, that these descriptions have had to be "translated" by the experiencer into a language familiar to his or her ordinary experience.

Hence a warning! It is no good believing in "other worlds" and "life hereafter" and other such phenomena just because someone has told of such things. Their experiences are of little value as more than "hints" to us—until such time as we have experiences ourselves with which to compare them.

*

There is a tendency to think of such experiences as remote, "mad" and confined to special people. In certain forms—perhaps crude and elementary and "unearned"—they are not so remote.

Alcohol can enable a person "to get away from himself"; drugs can take a person on a "trip" out of the ordinary realms of self-consciousness, space and time. (The drawback to both of these "artificial" methods is that they are not the result of training and effort and discipline—quite the opposite. Thus the mind has not been prepared to understand them and often cannot cope with their after-effects. Ordinarily, there is no control.)

And then there are the people who relate para-normal experiences

—for example, "out of the body" experiences when under anaesthetic or when they are seriously ill and may be near to death.

Self-induced trance states reveal all manner of visions and revelations, but they are rarely "pure" because they are frequently distorted by desires and fears in the mind of the participant. Even at a very ordinary level, dreams are remembered as illogical and extraordinary. In all these cases, there is experience of states of mind where the physical laws of matter, space and time are suspended.

As suggested above, when the experiences are artificial or accidental, they are only of value as hints. If they are engineered, claimed and used to satisfy "my" desires or alleviate "my" fears, they are apt to have unpleasant repercussions and they have nothing to do with religious discipline, the search for truth, spiritual realization, achieved higher states of consciousness nor "earning a living".

The great temptation with them (the "devil" aspect of them) is that the aspirant claims the powers for himself and uses them to gratify himself.

In extreme cases, there is the danger of total loss of control so that the mind is irretrievably "possessed".

*

We may also recognize other "out of this world" experiences which are quite different and hold no dangers.

When I am "in love", I *know* it. I know how it compares with being "out of love", and I may realize how such a state may be "earned". The song of a bird on a spring morning, the touch of a gentle hand, the beauty of a natural scene, a piece of music really listened to, a church service entered into wholeheartedly, the perfume of a flower or the scent of the sea, a poem responded to, a delicious taste—they can all "transport" me, out of myself. For timeless moments, the receptive mind is filled with "melting" emotions— of awe, wonder, gratitude, love, compassion—and I am "whole". Here there can be the sense of "holiness". It is as if all that ever has been and all that ever will be is contained in a timeless and perfect moment.

Are these "hints" also?

They are still actually "of this world" and often they seem to happen accidentally—but could they be intimations of eternity and immortality?

Heart, head and senses are in perfect harmony; the sense of "me" dies; the mind ceases its machinations; "I" transcend. It could be said that with "feet on the ground", the duality of "right" and "left" so balanced that the mind is still and centred and the "I" lifted out of involvement with belief and desire, the cross of suffering is transformed into a cross of "love and glory".

In such moments, the mind may acknowledge or "repent" and may realise ("real-i-se") "who I am". It will depend on the work that has been done to earn the experience.

*

So, the clue to the "mystical" experience lies in the fact that such states occur in a realm where there is a suspension of time and location.

Birth and death of the body are in time and in this world of matter. Mind beset with desires and fears, worldly concerns and pursuits, is bound to the body, bound to past and future, here and there.

But mind released from serving "me"? May it not discover an entirely different dispensation? Perhaps the "eternal now" and the "everywhere-and-everything-all-at-once"?

*

Before Abraham was, I am.

(John, 8:58)

*

And "I"?

I watch and wait—observing this life, responding to need, waiting for "resurrection" and "ascension".

I do not have to believe anything that passes for belief in this world . . . I just believe . . . "*in* God".

*

My God, my God, why hast thou forsaken me?

(Mark, 15:34)

*

No one can ever prove to me that there is a "god".

Throughout my life, my mind can give credence to many beliefs, adopt them and live according to them. It can also entertain many doubts, be plagued by them, and suffer for them.

I can believe there is a "god"; I can doubt it.

But all this believing and doubting may be the opposite of becoming "pure in heart" or as "a little child". To do this, I may have to give up all claim to this life being mine and "die to myself". And in the process, all my beliefs and doubts will die also. All that will remain will be "faith".

Faith in what?

Myself?

No.

Faith in the world as I think I know it?

No.

Faith in anything I think I know?

No.

Just faith . . . not in any known thing, but in what my mind may be pleased to call "God".

When I am no more of this body and no more of this mind, where am I?

*

The most sacred of ceremonies to the Christian is Communion. As the aspirant approaches the step to the altar (both a sacrificial table and a tomb) he approaches to partake of a mystical experience.

Taken literally, the words of the ritual suggest that the communicant is "eating the body" and "drinking the blood" of the Christ, in "remembrance".

There are echoes here of parallel primitive practices in which the participant sought to acquire the powers of other beings and spirits. In essence, we may perhaps say that the symbolic ritual in

Christianity carries the same connotation—of aspiring to and acquiring the characteristics and qualities of the Christ example.

But perhaps, at a transcendental or "higher mystical" level, Communion represents a total surrender or sacrifice—so that "I" am given up to, enter into oneness with, commune with . . . "God", "Our Father".

*

In that, for each aspirant, the ceremony should be a "secret" and mystical experience, it is not for us to debate or speculate about what happens in Communion.

It is for the Christian who has been confirmed to discover for himself or herself.

*

Meanwhile . . . what happens to me, *only experience can tell.*

I may get my experience through dedicated pursuit of the religious ideal or through the most obsessive pursuit of worldly pleasures. Who can say whether one course is better or worse then the other?

It is how we interpret and learn from our experience that matters. They say there is no short-cut to heaven.

St. Luke suggests (15:7) that "joy shall be in heaven over one sinner that repenteth, more than over ninety and nine just persons, which need no repentance."

Whatever my origins, my advantages, my talents, my flaws and shortcomings, whatever my disposition and my inclinations . . . my experience in life will be particular to me, and how I interpret it and learn from it will be particular to me. In this respect—what each experiences and *what each makes of it*—all are equal, not one more privileged than another.

*

It is not what happens to me on the "journey" that matters—it is what I make of it.

*

Jesus said: Become passers-by.

(Thomas, Log. 42)

137

Ten

*Go ye therefore, and teach all nations, baptizing them in the name
of the Father, and of the Son, and of the Holy Ghost:*
*Teaching them to observe all things whatsoever I have commanded
you: and, lo, I am with you alway, even unto the end of the world.
Amen.*

(Matthew, 28:19, 20)

*

And so,
there was a conception and a birth—and I came into this world.
I am—for a duration.
And then,
death comes to *me*, and I, without a mind to know with, and
without a body to sense with, leave this world.

*

We each of us make our journey through life and to the mind
that knows only the passing time of the body, it seems like "the
swift flight of a lone sparrow". Bound to the laws governing
exchange of energy and cycles of process, we are moved by desire—
getting and begetting, spending and being spent, conserving and
wasting, suffering ("allowing") joy and sorrow. We witness and
experience continuous change.

And yet, strangely, our lives can seem timeless and to the essential
centre of ourselves we are mysteriously constant and changeless,
ageless and untouched by all experience, as if we never "grew up"
and have never grown older, a presence which is unknown and
unknowing and to which nothing belongs.

138

And when it comes, surely death will be as innocent and virgin as seems the conception?

It means nothing to my mind.

It may be a *cliché* (but it is the nature of *clichés* that they are truisms) but naked we came into the world and naked we will leave it. We brought nothing with us; nor is there anything we can take with us when we depart.

Along the way of the journey we will gather a great deal; we will discover many amazing things; we will be puzzled by many problems and mysteries; we will listen to wonderful stories; we will find joy and sorrow; we may be inspired to remarkable achievements and live a full and active life; or we may find that ours is a quiet and uneventful course; or we may be doomed to more than what seems a fair share of misfortune, disadvantage and difficulty. (The Christian doctrine has very little to say about possible reasons for the varied and seemingly arbitrary fates of different people).

And, on occasions, we may pause and ask:

What is it all *for*?

*

Such a question may lead us to search for the answers to the many confusing enigmas of our lives.

If so, then we seek to discover others who share the same questions—in the hope that they will be of some assistance and be company for us in our quest.

And we will come to hear about special people who appear to have (or had) the answers and who are (or have been) willing— sometimes eagerly, sometimes reluctantly—to impart their knowledge. Some have gone out into the world to spread their message; others have led secluded lives and only taught those who have made considerable effort to find them.

These teachers—sages, saints, prophets, priests, gurus, mystics, sheikhs, rabbis, and so on—have existed from time to time in different parts of the world for as long as history has been recorded— and beyond, according to verbal tradition.

They have spoken, and speak now, to different cultures and different races, and sometimes their teachings, their interpretations of truth, seem to be contradictory.

But, in one respect, they all have something in common—they have over and over again used stories to convey the subtleties of their message.

Why should this be?

What is the special nature of *fiction* that it should be so frequently employed as a vehicle to transmit special knowledge? Would not *fact* be so much more simple and direct? After all, is it not fact that the mind assumes to be synonymous with truth?

Perhaps it has something to do with the ability of fiction to suggest; its flexibility; its neutrality in that it allows the recipient to take what he wants from it without ruining and distorting it? Fiction conveys meaning whereas facts uncompromisingly try to tell.

What we call "facts" (that which is "made" or "done") are "of this world" and are *learnt* "in this world". They constitute a report or explanation, according to man, of what has been or is going on in the world of phenomena. And "facts" are notoriously subject to dispute and change of fashion. They are modified by new learning, by re-interpretation, according to the views of particular men using the various languages that *they have invented*.

Perhaps the "higher truths" can never be stated as "facts"? Perhaps "facts" are really "fiction"? And perhaps what we call "fiction", if it is informed by insight and profound knowledge, is the most effective way of hinting at the truth? This suggests that the ordinary, logical mind cannot *learn* the truth because the truth cannot be stated as "fact".

In other words, if truth is made manifest, it is known within the individual at a deeper level of understanding and is "beyond" the limits of human communication.

*

Let me suppose that I am in a world of constant darkness, of eternal night.

And then let me suppose further that I am inspired with the idea that there could be light.

For such an inspiration to have taken place, there must be a preconception, from "beyond" the experience and learning of the ordinary mind, of the meaning of "light". For how can the mind accept an idea about something unless "somewhere, somehow" it is already known?

I may be "inspired" as I become aware of the form of the idea— but the inspiration has to meet with, be reciprocated by, be compatible with, be aligned with, my ability to comprehend the meaning. Otherwise I could not cognize the idea's "message". (Just as the male chromosomes, carried by the sperm penetrating the "darkness of the womb", "find" and pair off with their complementary, dormant but waiting, female chromosomes, delivering the "message" of a potential new creation, forming the bi-lateral blueprint for a new and independent existence.)

It is as though inspiration is "memory illuminated".

*

Inspiration is a re-membering, a revealing or discovering (un-covering) of truth—which is already there "unseen".

Only later may it become fact for the world at large.

*

And so, perhaps, in the world of continuous darkness, I seek for confirmation of my inspiration that there could be "light".

But it is perpetual darkness and there is no vision, no revelation of "light" . . . until the clouds thin and part and the pale, silver light of the rising moon bathes the earth and I am confirmed in my inspiration, my "divine message".

I *see* what I think is "light" and I believe in it.

But do I comprehend it?

Later still, I may discover that the "fact" of light is only a relative "truth" about light. The moon's light is but a reflection; the moon itself is not the source of the light; it has none of its own.

I realize that I cannot see the "light"; I only know it is there because it is being reflected by substance.

So where is the source—the sun? I cannot see it within the field of my present vision. What is the sun? I do not know it.

*

The world—the form of it and the per-form-ance of it—is a "fact" for me. It can be seen all around.

But is it perhaps also a reflection?

The reflection of what? "God's reflection"?

It has no light of its own; does it hint at an unseen source?

*

I may live out my night believing in the reflected light of the moon. I can see dimly by it; it illuminates my world and my living sufficiently for worldly purposes. I do not need to bother where the light comes from; it is enough that it is there.

Will it be of any value to me if someone tells me the "fact" that an unseen sun is the real source of the light? I can see by moonlight and so I can ignore the possibility. Unless, that is, I respect the intelligence of my informant more than I value my own. In that case, I may adopt my informant's assertion, accept the belief, and thus put my trust in that which I do not know for myself, simply because I am persuaded.

If, however, it is suggested to me that the moonlight is but a pale reflection . . . and that suggestion re-minds me of something that I once knew . . .

What if I am inspired by *memory* of the sun?

*

I am he who sees and believes in the fact and evidence of the moonlight.

And I am he who remembers the direct light of the sun which reason tells me must be the real light.

Can my mind hold both the "outer truth" of my senses and the "inner truth" of my intuition?

Can my mind serve both simultaneously?

Or can the mind comprehend that they are both "true", one being subject or partner to the other?

*

I am he who is born into the world, grows in the world, lives in the world, believes in the world, ages in the world and dies in the world.

And I am he within who witnesses the world, does not become involved in the world, never changes, does not grow older, and seems, strangely, never to have been born.

How can I be both?

*

There is a story that Jesus is reported to have told:

. . . A certain man had two sons:

And the younger of them said to his father, Father, give me the portion of goods that falleth to me. And he divided unto them his living.

And not many days after the younger son gathered all together, and took his journey into a far country, and there wasted his substance with riotous living.

And when he had spent all, there arose a mighty famine in that land; and he began to be in want.

And he went and joined himself to a citizen of that country; and he sent him into his fields to feed swine.

And he would fain have filled his belly with the husks that the swine did eat; and no man gave unto him.

And when he came to himself, he said, How many hired servants of my father's have bread enough and to spare, and I perish with hunger!

I will arise and go to my father, and will say unto him, Father, I have sinned against heaven, and before thee,

And am no more worthy to be called thy son: make me as one of thy hired servants.

And he arose, and came to his father. But when he was yet a great way off, his father saw him, and had compassion, and ran, and fell on his neck, and kissed him.

143

And the son said unto him, Father, I have sinned against heaven, and in thy sight, and am no more worthy to be called thy son.

But the father said to his servants, Bring forth the best robe, and put it on him; and put a ring on his hand, and shoes on his feet:

And bring hither the fatted calf, and kill it; and let us eat, and be merry:

For this my son was dead, and is alive again; he was lost, and is found. And they began to be merry.

Now his elder son was in the field: and as he came and drew nigh to the house, he heard musick and dancing.

And he called one of the servants, and asked what these things meant.

And he said unto him, Thy brother is come; and thy father hath killed the fatted calf, because he hath received him safe and sound.

And he was angry, and would not go in: therefore came his father out, and intreated him.

And he answering said to his father, Lo, these many years do I serve thee, neither transgressed I at any time thy commandment: and yet thou never gavest me a kid, that I might make merry with my friends:

But as soon as this thy son was come, which hath devoured thy living with harlots, thou hast killed for him the fatted calf.

And he said unto him, Son, thou art ever with me, and all that I have is thine.

It was meet that we should make merry, and be glad: for this thy brother was dead, and is alive again; and was lost, and is found.

(Luke, 15:11–32)

*

This story is one of the most cherished in the Christian faith religion. It has become known as "The Parable of the Prodigal Son", and it is held to demonstrate certain basic Christian principles for living a "good" life. Its strength seems to lie in its ability to reflect the truth about the state of man in this world.

Commonly, it has been interpreted simply as an exhortation that men should turn away from their sins, stop wasting their real potential in loose and selfish living, and to return to the "father" —a synonym for the one "god".

144

As such, it is certainly a vivid and effective tale.

However, is that the full significance of it?

The strength of fiction, as we have suggested, is that when it is informed by profound knowledge it can speak simultaneously to different levels of comprehension. It cannot be confined to one interpretation.

Can we explore it further?

I wonder why it is never called "The Parable of the Son Who Stayed at Home"?

*

He seems to have a role as significant as the other son.

By our standards of fairness, he seems to have had a rough deal! And, what is more, he thought so too.

Who is this other son, this first-born?

Is it not strange that the Christian nowadays, identifying readily with the fate of the younger brother, tends to consider the elder so little?

*

Could the story be validly interpreted as having something to do with the dual aspect of the mind?

For example, perhaps the two sons have something to do with the dual aspect of "I"—the one which believes the evidence of the senses and identifies itself with the body and the world, and the other which stands apart, constant and unchanging, uninvolved, simply witnessing the "play" of life?

*

The father had two sons; he "divided his *living*" between them.

The younger son (born later) took his share of the father's living (he had not earned it himself) and went on a journey to a far country. There he spent all that he had been given ("wasted his substance") and began to be in want. He "joined himself" to "a citizen" of that country. And "*no man gave unto him*". And "when he came to himself" (remembered?), he decided ("I will arise") to return home and say to his father, "Make *me* a servant".

145

The elder son never went to the far country. He stayed at his father's house. And the father "came out" and reassured him that he was always with the father and that everything the father had was his.

*

Am I the "prodigal"?
(Strangely, although "prodigal" has the connotation of reckless wasting, its root meaning has to do with "driving or setting in motion, for or on behalf of". Might this not suggest that there was nothing "wrong", wilful or selfish, in going to the far country? Perhaps the younger son's experience of his journey had a purpose which he had to understand.)
Am I then he who emerged from my mother's womb with my portion of living, who is now making the journey through life, wasting my substance, "dead and lost" already, unless and until I decide to "arise" and return whence I came?
Or, am I the elder brother who never enters the far country but works in the fields at home?
Which am I?
Who am I?

*

Could I be *both*?
After "division of the living", the brothers never speak to each other nor meet. It could be that with our logical minds we are apt to assume that they both co-existed in time. But the older brother's not going into the far country but staying at home could suggest not only separation in location but also in time. This would suggest that "I" could be both brothers—but not *in* or *at* the same time. "At home" I am in eternal time; "in the far country" I am always moving and travelling in chronological time—either away from, or far from, or towards "home"—until I leave this world.

*

And, *above all*, who is the father?
When "he came to himself", he remembered.

*

No one will ever satisfactorily tell me directly the answers. Only I can recognize the truth as my mind reflects it clearly through observation of my own experience.

However, the stories that I hear of other men's experience—both mundane and inspired—can point the way, give me hints, encourage me to continue the search and may illuminate and structure what I vaguely already recognize and remember.

Only *I* watch and listen.

And only *I* can resurrect (be raised away from the country of the "dead") by my decision to ascend ("I will arise").

*

Follow me; and let the dead bury their dead.

(Matthew, 8:22)

*

If I want to know what I look like, do I not require a mirror or some other smooth reflecting surface in which to see my image?

And, if I wish to see that image objectively, do I not have to remember to "stand back" and cease to be identified and involved with the reflected image, ceasing to be deluded by the belief that that is who I am? Does not the image then become a "stranger"?

Could the Prodigal Son appreciate his home—until he had moved away from it, become estranged from the far country, and then remembered what he had left behind?

Is it not also significant that the Son Who Stayed At Home was passive and perfectly content until the adventurous brother had left the far country?

Once stirred into activity and angered, he stays out "in the field" and will not go into the house. Whereupon the father "comes out" and reassures him, "Thou art ever with me; and all that I have is thine."

*

If there is no question—then there is no need for an answer.

If there is a question—then it is the answer asking to be remembered.

147

It is as if the question is the moon-reflection in the night sky of the answer that lies in the sun.

And I am the one who experiences the question and remembers the answer here in the earth-darkness of my mind.

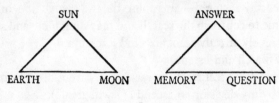

*

When you make the two one, you shall become sons of Man, and when you say: "Mountain, be moved", it will be moved.

*

For as long as I continue my journey through the far country of life, I will, on occasions, have glimmering memories of my true home.

Perhaps the sounds of music . . . perhaps the scent of a flower . . . perhaps a falling leaf . . . perhaps a distant horizon . . . perhaps a loving caress . . . will remind me for a moment, and my breath will come as a sigh, and the tension will disappear.

Then I will say to myself: "That is heaven!" And my heart responds and tells me that that is how it really is.

Such are the hints which call me and give me hope.

Such are the intimations—but I must remember that they are the *reflections* of truth in my mind, not the truth itself.

*

I am separated by the time of this far country from the state of bliss, but for moments I am bathed in it.

These individual experiences are entirely mine. No one else can have them for me.

The word "individual" means "not divisible", "not divided", "not seeing two".

For such transcendental experiences to take place it is *necessary* that I should first have been divided or separated from it, for how else can I *know* what it is to come back into the state of union?

How can I "know God" unless I have first been separated?

In the Christian ceremony of Holy Communion is the symbolic enactment of deciding: "I will arise and go to my father". "Decide" means to "cut off from" which in turn suggests that I can only go to "the father" if I am willing to cut off from this "far country", this world.

*

For ONE to exist to itself there has to appear to be TWO, the creator and the created.

If there is not TWO, there can only be the ONE NO-THING.

And when ONE begets TWO, there is immediately THREE (the ONE and the apparent TWO).

There can be no active without passive; and neither can "proceed" to any purpose without the third, the condition which governs the relationship and product of the process.

The ONE reflects upon itself in order to know that it IS.

In such a way may we consider the essential TRINITY which is the fulcrum of the Christ story (and which with various labels is at the heart of all religion).

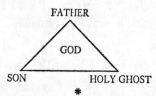

*

Christianity may give *me* many laws and many concepts and beliefs. Christianity may instruct *me* how I should behave and should not behave (be-have). Christianity may govern *me* throughout my life—if I believe in it.

As such, Christianity may become a secure and welcome haven for *me* when the journey is difficult. To aspire to becoming a "good" Christian may not be all that easy—but at least it gives *me* something to aim at.

149

But is that enough to provide understanding as to who *I am*? Will I realize who Christ *is*? Will I come to *know* God?

In the end, if I do not understand the meaning of the stories for *my-self*—and make them *whole* within *my-self*—then, no matter how hopeful I may be, *I* will not knowingly return home. You cannot go home for me; *I* must go there for *my-self*.

You may equip me and point the way—but *I* have to travel.

*

The foxes have holes, and the birds of the air have nests; but the Son of man hath not where to lay his head.

(Matthew, 8:20)

*

We have spoken of this search for truth as a journey into the labyrinth or maze.

It appeared at first that we were apparently "outside" it and were endeavouring to reach the "mystery" at the centre. But would it not now seem more appropriate to consider that in the beginning we were already at the dimensionless centre, "the far country", and that we are actually trying to find our way *out*?

Only when I get out will I know who and what I am?

Only then could the "father" say: " . . . For this my son was dead, and is alive again; he was lost, and is found."

*

Then I may see that once I know the way out of the labyrinth, then I will no longer be lost and it will no longer be a maze. It will not then matter whether I am inside it or outside it. If I wish, I may be able to come and go as I will.

*

If I was "sent" by the "Father" into this body and mind, then I must both do His work and find the way back to Him, aided by divine knowledge (Holy Ghost) in memory, aware that His desire to be reunited is manifest in what I experience as Love.

*

This Love, therefore, is not something to be directed towards something outside the self but is rather something that manifests at the very heart of self and, once released in full measure, flows out to embrace all things.

Perhaps we could call this "centre-that-is-everywhere" by the name "God"? And perhaps it is to this mysterious power that a Christian may pray.

This is a long way from the concept of "God" as a divine something, somewhere "out there", separate and aloof, to whom we are encouraged to believe we can talk and beg favours.

When a Christian prays, to whom is he speaking? To "God"—or to himself?

If I am speaking to myself, what can there possibly be to say?—unless it be that in memory the divine knowledge, the Holy Ghost, moves in *me* and *I* utter words and am reminded of things forgotten.

Here indeed is inspiration.

Here indeed the mind becomes receptive to the messenger—the "angel of God".

Perhaps the function of real prayer is not to be asking for "things" to be changed—nor even to be asking for strength to accept them as they are. Perhaps prayer is essentially *listening* . . . to the sound of what I am speaking; and *waiting* . . . for inspiration.

Only with such disposition of the mind can the "two sons" be in correct relationship with "the father".

Thus prayer must be the most intensely personal and individual experience of the religious life.

*

For, when we pray—who is speaking?
I am.
And when we pray—who is listening?
I am.
Prayer is the link or the bridge that unites the "two sons" in the house of "the father".

*

151

I am Alpha and Omega, the beginnning and the ending . . .
(Revelation, 1:8)

*

We have only touched here and there on the Christ story.

And we have questioned—especially the validity of assumed belief—not with the intention of spreading doubt but with confidence in the ability of the healthy individual of today to exercise the intelligence required to overcome superstition and, maybe, to encourage those who baulk at the blandishments of established religion to take a fresh look.

The Christ story can be the most wonderful and illuminating testament and confirmation—but only, we suggest, if it is related to observation of the mind's experience and only if it is under-stood at levels deeper than those most immediately attractive to the ordinary workings of the mind—the literal, the logical, the scientific, the exercise of theoretical debate.

Today, there can be nothing more important or urgent than wider understanding of the meaning of leading the religious life— that it is a living, working, daily concern and not just a periodic performance of ritual. The form of religion—the dogma, the ceremony, the repetitive recitations, the "blind" belief—can be so self-deluding. Certainly it can be a comfort and a refuge—and, temporarily, there need be no harm in that. But lulling complacency can so easily mask and suppress valid disquiet. (The more fanatical the evangelist, the more likely he is suppressing disquiet within himself.) For if I am disquieted, it can well be that the inner "conscience" is suspecting the self-delusion and is yearning for the truth. "Make-believe" must always be the playing of a self-confidence trick on oneself.

Misunderstood, religion can so easily become for the young a "dream" or a "cause" to throw themselves into, for the middle-aged a "refuge" or a "debate", and for the old a "desperate hope".

Understood, it can be an inspiration for youth, strength for middle age and conviction for the old.

*

We have made the journey here.

Are we content to stay here?

Or do we want to go back home?

Once the return journey is started, there is no turning back. And it is very unlikely to be "roses all the way".

But, having forsaken the far country, there can be no journey more rewarding or worthwhile.

*

Just suppose that at my birth, I "died"; and that at my death, I am "re-born" . . .

*

The disciples said to Jesus: Tell us how our end will be.

Jesus said: Have you then discovered the beginning so that you inquire about the end? For where the beginning is, there shall be the end. Blessed is he who shall stand at the beginning, and he shall know the end and he shall not taste death.

(Thomas, Log. 18)

*

Prayer, in the Christian faith, ends with a single word; it means "so be it". Its secret is in its sound—and just as the beginning was the Word, so is the continuing and the end.

AMEN

*

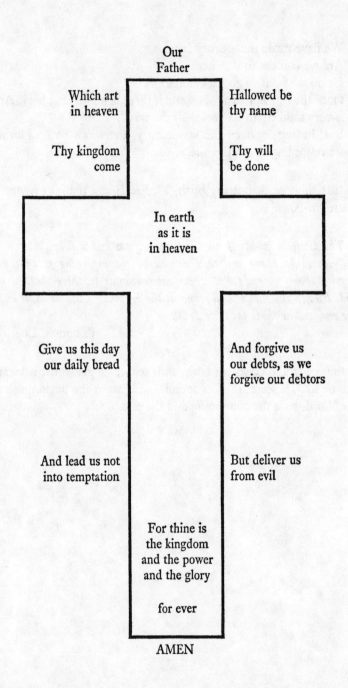

Our
Father

Which art
in heaven

Hallowed be
thy name

Thy kingdom
come

Thy will
be done

In earth
as it is
in heaven

Give us this day
our daily bread

And forgive us
our debts, as we
forgive our debtors

And lead us not
into temptation

But deliver us
from evil

For thine is
the kingdom
and the power
and the glory

for ever

AMEN